New Directions for
Child and Adolescent
Development

Elena L.
Grigorenko
EDITOR-IN-CHIEF

William Damon
FOUNDING EDITOR

Perspectives on Creativity Development

Baptiste Barbot

EDITOR

Number 151 • Spring 2016
Jossey-Bass
San Francisco

PERSPECTIVES ON CREATIVITY DEVELOPMENT
Baptiste Barbot (ed.)
New Directions for Child and Adolescent Development, no. 151
Elena L. Grigorenko, Editor-in-Chief

Microfilm copies of issues and articles are available in 16 mm and 35 mm, as well as microfiche in 105 mm, through University Microfilms, Inc., 300 North Zeeb Road, Ann Arbor, Michigan 48106-1346.

ISSN 1520-3247   electronic ISSN 1534-8687

NEW DIRECTIONS FOR CHILD AND ADOLESCENT DEVELOPMENT is part of The Jossey-Bass Education Series and is published quarterly by Wiley Subscription Services, Inc., a Wiley company, at Jossey-Bass, One Montgomery Street, Suite 1200, San Francisco, CA 94104-4594. Postmaster: Send address changes to New Directions for Child and Adolescent Development, Jossey-Bass, One Montgomery Street, Suite 1200, San Francisco, CA 94104-4594.

New Directions for Child and Adolescent Development is indexed in Cambridge Scientific Abstracts (CSA/CIG), CHID: Combined Health Information Database (NIH), Contents Pages in Education (T&F), Educational Research Abstracts Online (T&F), Embase (Elsevier), ERIC Database (Education Resources Information Center), Index Medicus/MEDLINE (NLM), Linguistics & Language Behavior Abstracts (CSA/CIG), Psychological Abstracts/PsycINFO (APA), Social Services Abstracts (CSA/CIG), SocINDEX (EBSCO), and Sociological Abstracts (CSA/CIG).

INDIVIDUAL SUBSCRIPTION RATE (in USD): $89 per year US/Can/Mex, $113 rest of world; institutional subscription rate: $416 US, $456 Can/Mex, $490 rest of world. Single copy rate: $29. Electronic only–all regions: $89 individual, $416 institutional; Print & Electronic–US: $98 individual, $500 institutional; Print & Electronic–Canada/Mexico: $98 individual, $540 institutional; Print & Electronic–Rest of World: $122 individual, $574 institutional.

COVER PHOTOGRAPHS: ©iStock.com/paulaphoto (top); ©iStock.com/vm (middle); ©iStock.com/ericsphotography (bottom)

EDITORIAL CORRESPONDENCE should be e-mailed to the editor-in-chief: Elena L. Grigorenko (elena.grigorenko@yale.edu).

Jossey-Bass Web address: www.josseybass.com

CONTENTS

Preface: Perspectives on Creativity Development   7
Baptiste Barbot
This editorial note provides a brief context for the volume and acknowledge all the contributions.

1. Creativity Doesn't Develop in a Vacuum   9
John Baer
This article discusses how creativity is necessarily tied to content and should therefore be understood as a domain-specific entity as it develops.

2. Pretend Play: Antecedent of Adult Creativity   21
Sandra W. Russ
In this article, pretend play in young children is discussed as an important antecedent of adult creativity given the commonality of cognitive and affective processes involved.

3. "Peaks, Slumps, and Bumps": Individual Differences in the Development of Creativity in Children and Adolescents   33
Baptiste Barbot, Todd I. Lubart, Maud Besançon
This article reviews and interprets creativity slumps in light of the interaction between individual-level resources, task-specific demands, and environmental influences.

4. The Cross-Cultural Invariance of Creative Cognition: A Case Study of Creative Writing in U.S. and Russian College Students   47
Sergey A. Kornilov, Tatiana V. Kornilova, Elena L. Grigorenko
This empirical study offers a psychometric approach to understand how culture may shape the structure and development of creativity.

5. Inhibitory Control as a Core Process of Creative Problem Solving and Idea Generation from Childhood to Adulthood   61
Mathieu Cassotti, Marine Agogué, Anaëlle Camarda, Olivier Houdé, Grégoire Borst
This article reviews research from the field of developmental cognitive neuroscience showing the role of inhibitory control in creative problem solving.

6. Creativity Development in Adolescence: Insight from 73
Behavior, Brain, and Training Studies
Sietske W. Kleibeuker, Carsten K. W. De Dreu, Eveline A. Crone
In this article, the development of creativity in adolescence is interpreted in light of adolescent's brain and behavioral control processes development.

7. Creative Aspirations or Pipe Dreams? Toward 85
Understanding Creative Mortification in Children and
Adolescents
Ronald A. Beghetto, Anna E. Dilley
This article introduces an empirically testable model of creative mortification and its influence on the development of creativity of children and adolescents.

Commentary: Overview of Developmental Perspectives on 97
Creativity and the Realization of Potential
Mark A. Runco
This commentary underscores some of the key ideas in the volume and pinpoints issues with the concept of Big C creativity, lack of cultural relativity, and inappropriate testing of divergent thinking.

Commentary: The Development of Creativity—Ability, 111
Motivation, and Potential
Paul J. Silvia, Alexander P. Christensen, Katherine N. Cotter
This commentary challenges the concept of creative potential (vs. creativity) outlined in the volume and organizes the contributions in a proposed *ability* × *motivation* framework of creativity development.

INDEX 121

Preface: Perspectives on Creativity Development

Twenty years ago, *New Directions for Child and Adolescent Development* (NDCAD) published an influential volume on the development of creativity (1996, vol. 72) under the editorship of Mark Runco, featuring landmark contributions such as those by Robert Albert, Sandra Russ, and Ruth Richards. Two decades later, it is evident that much has happened in this line of work at the intersection of creativity research and developmental science. Up to this point, creativity development was already understood as a nonlinear process (illustrated by "slumps" research triggered by Torrance, 1968), which begins early in life (as manifested in play and other antecedents of creativity described early on by developmentalists). As the environmental and sociocultural roots of creativity began to be acknowledged (e.g., Amabile, 1996), so did its multifaceted and partly domain-specific nature (e.g., Baer, 1991; Sternberg & Lubart, 1991). This had important implications for understanding creativity development.

What did the past two decades bring into this picture? Certainly a great deal of depth to the various "facets" of creativity development, which some may interpret as a fragmentation of the field. These advances occurred at the same time as the emergence of (developmental) neuroscience perspectives on creativity that have greatly colored the theoretical landscape in recent years. This volume attempts to represent and integrate these various perspectives on the development of creativity, a challenging, yet very much needed endeavor for researchers and practitioners who seek to promote creativity development in children and adolescents.

Specifically, Baer (Article 1) makes the case for the domain specificity of creativity as the basic condition for understanding its development and for nurturing it in children and adolescents. Russ (Article 2) outlines the antecedent of adult creativity that can be found in the pretend play of young children, because cognitive and affective processes in play are also important for later creative production. Together with Besançon and Lubart (Barbot, Besançon, & Lubart, Article 3), we interpret classic creativity "slumps" and other evidence of the nonlinearity of creativity development in light of the interaction between individual-level resources, task-specific demands, and environmental influences. In their empirical study, Kornilov, Kornilova, and Grigorenko (Article 4) offer a psychometric approach to understanding how culture may shape the structure and development of creativity throughout the life span. Rooted in the emerging developmental cognitive neuroscience approach to creativity, Cassotti, Agogué, Camarda, Houdé, and Borst (Article 5) present evidence of the central role inhibitory control has in creative problem solving and idea generation from childhood to adulthood. Also based on recent neuroscience evidence, Kleibeuker, De Dreu, and Crone (Article 6) summarize studies that have demonstrated a dramatic development of creativity in adolescence, interpreted in light of the development of adolescents' brain and behavioral control processes. Beghetto and Dilley (Article 7) focus on how experiences, especially negative experiences, influence the development of creativity of children and adolescents and how these experiences can lead to what they coined "creative mortification". Finally, commentaries by Runco and by Silvia, Christensen, and Cotter provide a very different, yet surprisingly efficient integration of these multiple perspectives on creativity development. Indeed, despite their apparent heterogeneity, the contributions in this volume all outline some common, important directions for research in the field that are further put forth in the commentaries.

In sum, this 20th anniversary of NDCAD volume on creativity development not only represents some of the main directions of the field in the past 20 years; it also provides an agenda for creativity researchers and developmentalists for the next few decades. Given the renewed interest for the study of creativity development and suggested directions presented in this volume, I am looking forward to what another two decades of research in this area will bring.

Author Notes

I am grateful to all authors for their wonderful contributions to this volume, as well as to all reviewers, the NDCAD board, Cheri Stahl (NDCAD administrator), Jens F. Beckmann (action editor for this issue), and Elena Grigorenko (NDCAD editor-in-chief).

Baptiste Barbot
Editor

References

Amabile, T. M. (1996). *Creativity in context*. Boulder, CO: Westview.

Baer, J. (1991). Generality of creativity across performance domains. *Creativity Research Journal, 4*(1), 23–39.

Sternberg, R. J., & Lubart, T. I. (1991). An investment theory of creativity and its development. *Human Development, 34*(1), 1–31.

Torrance, E. P. (1968). A longitudinal examination of the fourth grade slump in creativity. *Gifted Child Quarterly, 12*(4), 195–199.

BAPTISTE BARBOT *is an assistant professor in psychology at the Department of Psychology, Pace University, New York, NY, and an adjunct assistant professor at the Child Study Center, Yale University, New Haven, CT.*

Baer, J. (2016). Creativity doesn't develop in a vacuum. In B. Barbot (Ed.), *Perspectives on creativity development. New Directions for Child and Adolescent Development, 151*, 9–20.

1

Creativity Doesn't Develop in a Vacuum

John Baer

Abstract

The skills, knowledge, attitudes, motivations, and personality traits that lead to creative thinking and creative behavior do not exist—and do not develop—in a vacuum. They are inextricably tied to content, to domains, in particular, and they therefore vary by domains. The more we learn about creativity, the more we discover how domain specific creativity is. This means we cannot nurture creativity, or any of the skills or attributes that contribute to creativity, without thinking about content. One cannot become physically fit by doing just one kind of exercise that trains a single set of muscles; all-around fitness requires diverse exercises that use and train many different sets of muscles. So it is with creativity. Different domains require different creativity-relevant skills, knowledge, attitudes, motivations, and personality traits. If we want to help children and adolescents become more creative, then we need to attend to the domains we use in the development of creativity. © 2016 Wiley Periodicals, Inc.

T he development of creativity is something almost all educators agree is important, but most creativity educators would argue that disturbingly little is being done to promote creativity (Baer & Kaufman, 2012; Beghetto, 2013; Besançon, Lubart, & Barbot, 2013; Plucker & Beghetto, 2015). In an introductory essay for a special issue of *Psychology of Aesthetics, Creativity, and the Arts* on "Creativity and Education," a long-time observer of schools noted that:

> There are hundreds of books and thousands of articles on how to teach children to think creatively. If one walks into a classroom, however, one is not likely to see a lot of teaching for creative thinking. (Sternberg, 2015, p. 115)

Why the absence of creativity-focused education? Some will argue that the standards and accountability focus of recent decades have driven creativity education from schools. To the extent that this is true, it is based on a misunderstanding of both how to teach for creativity and how best to promote the acquisition of skills and knowledge (Baer, 1999, 2002). Creativity *requires* a great deal of domain-based skills and knowledge, so the need to meet content standards is not a barrier to creativity development (Baer, 2015); and the best ways to acquire domain-based skills and knowledge involve using them constructively and in diverse ways, which makes assignments to promote creative thinking natural allies with the goals of the content standards movement (Beghetto, Kaufman, & Baer, 2015).

Content standards like the Common Core are not—or should not be—roadblocks to teaching creative thinking skills. The obsession with testing that both preceded and now accompanies the Common Core, however, has become just such an obstacle:

> Another unfortunate misconception is the belief that we must be able to *measure* every outcome that we care about. Valid and meaningful assessment is hard, especially if we want to assess complex kinds of thinking, but the fact that we may not be able to test, in a standardized format, some of the things that we want to teach should not prevent us from teaching or valuing those things. For this reason, Common Core *testing* may be a genuine roadblock and the use of such tests for any high-stakes decisions (e.g., who gets a diploma, or who gets—or gets to keep—a teaching job) should be reconsidered, but that is no reason to avoid using the Common Core (or another set of rigorous content-based standards) as guides in education. We can (and should) teach things that matter whether or not we can test them adequately (Baer, in press-b).

The fact that creativity may be impossible to test in the kind of standardized format that will allow valid cross-district and cross-era comparisons does not mean that creativity in many domains cannot be assessed in any way. Experts in a domain can very reliably assess the creativity of artifacts produced in that domain, as Amabile and others have shown convincingly (Amabile, 1982, 1983, 1996; Baer, Kaufman, & Gentile, 2004). But attempts to assess creativity in a standardized format have had little success. As Csikszentmihalyi (2013) observed:

> If one turns to the literature of creativity research and asks the simple question: What is being measured? What is creativity? One soon realizes that the entire research enterprise moves on very thin ice. (p. 143)

Sawyer's (2012) summary of the results of more than a half century of work in creativity test development is similarly pessimistic:

> Different tests, each designed to measure creativity, often aren't correlated with one another, thus failing to demonstrate convergent validity. Another problem is that even though some of these tests correlate with creative achievement, the tests might in fact correlate with *all* achievement. Rather than measuring creativity, they might be measuring success and social achievement more generally—and IQ tests probably do a better job of that. (p. 61; original italics)

Attempts to assess creativity in a standardized way have mostly taken the form of divergent thinking tests, with the Torrance Tests the most widely used, but these tests have been under attack for many years for lack of validity. Anastasi wrote in 1982 that any "evidence of relation between the Torrance Tests and everyday-life criteria of creative achievement is meager" (p. 391), and a decade earlier Crockenberg (1972) reviewed the evidence that Torrance (1972a, 1972b) had offered for his tests and concluded that "given the creativity criteria used . . . [the results of his validity studies] should not be taken too seriously" (p. 35). Sternberg (1985) opined that "Such tests capture, at best, only the most trivial aspects of creativity" (p. 618). In 2009, Division 10 of the American Psychological Association (Psychology of Aesthetics, Creativity, and the Arts) held its first ever debate with the topic "Are the Torrance Tests still relevant in the 21st century?" (Baer, 2009; Kim, 2009).

There are many things that schools try to teach that cannot be assessed in standardized ways, however, and this assessment failure has not prevented schools from trying to teach those things anyway. What school mission statement doesn't say something about such hard-to-assess goals as creating socially responsible citizens, lifelong learners, and students who respect and value diversity? The fact that some kinds of skills, knowledge, attitudes, and traits are hard to measure (and especially hard to measure when the relevant skills, knowledge, attitudes, and traits that matter for creativity vary from domain to domain) is not a reason to abandon them as goals. If, like respect for diversity and other important goals, creativity is hard to assess, that is not a reason for schools to dismiss it as not worth promoting and teaching.

One problem that creativity education has faced—a self-imposed problem—is the erratic success of creativity training programs. Far too much creativity training has been time wasted, mostly because of poorly designed programs based on a fundamental misunderstanding of the nature of creativity (and its development).

Scott, Leritz, and Mumford (2004) conducted a quantitative meta-analysis of creativity training research covering a half century of research—70 published and peer-reviewed studies on the effectiveness of creativity training. There was good news: they found that "well-designed creativity training programs typically induce gains in performance" (p. 361). But there was also bad news, which was encapsulated in the phrase "*well-designed* creativity training programs."

What constituted good design, the kind that led to positive outcomes?

[M]ore successful programs were likely to focus on development of cognitive skills and the heuristics involved in skill application, using realistic exercises appropriate to the domain at hand. (p. 361)

The key issue was that the training exercises needed to be "appropriate to the domain at hand." Creativity training worked when the training and the goals of the training (and the ways the effectiveness of the training was assessed) were *in the same domain*. "The most clear-cut finding to emerge in the overall analysis was that the use of domain-based performance exercises was positively related ($r = .31$, $\beta = .35$) to effect size" (p. 380).

Barbot, Besançon, and Lubart (2011) suggested the need for an even tighter focus than domain specificity in arguing for *task* specificity: "the most effective training programs will be those tailored to enhance creativity in a specific domain, and even better in a specific task" (p. 130). This call for task or subdomain specificity echoes Pretz and McCollum's (2014) caution about the need for extremely domain-specific analyses: "Perhaps prior studies of domain-specific creativity were not specific enough" (p. 233) to uncover effects that more specific assessments might have revealed.

For those who have followed creativity research over the past two decades, these results should come as no surprise. It was almost two decades ago that the *Creativity Research Journal* published the only point–counterpoint debate it has ever featured. The topic of that 1998 debate was the domain specificity of creativity, and even the debater arguing for domain generality acknowledged that the outlook for domain generality was already looking rather grim:

Recent observers of the theoretical (Csikszentmihalyi, 1988) and empirical (Gardner, 1993; Runco, 1989; Sternberg & Lubart, 1995) creativity literature could reasonably assume that the debate is settled in favor of content specificity. In fact, Baer (1994a, 1994b, 1994c) provided convincing evidence that creativity is not only content specific but is also task specific within content areas. (Plucker, 1998, p. 179)

Research looking at actual creative performance has consistently shown that creativity in one domain does not predict creativity in other domains (see Baer, 1998b, 2010, 2013, 2016 for summaries of this research). In a typical experiment of this kind, researchers ask subjects (who have ranged from kindergarten age to adults) to create several different kinds of things in different domains. Creating short stories, collages, interesting math word problems, drawings, structures, paintings, and poems have been favorite tasks in these studies, although many other domains have been tapped as well. Experts in those domains rate them for creativity using Amabile's Consensual Assessment Technique (Amabile, 1983, 1996). The two sides of this debate make different key predictions, as summed up by Ivcevic (2007):

Domain generality would be supported by high intercorrelations among different creative behaviors and a common set of psychological descriptors for those behaviors, while domain specificity would be supported by relatively low correlations among different behaviors, and a diverging set of psychological descriptors of those behaviors. (p. 272)

The results have been consistent: low to nonexistent correlations between creativity ratings of subjects' creations in different domains.

Even research that has tried to find evidence for domain generality in performance assessments has found (as domain specificity predicts) only positive correlations on tasks in the same domains. For example, Conti, Coon, and Amabile (1996) had young adults in an introductory psychology class complete a total of four story-writing tasks (using different prompts) and three rather different kinds of art activities. The intercorrelations they reported among the story-writing creativity ratings were indeed both high and statistically significant, suggesting that these measures were largely measures of the same domain-based ability. The correlations among the ratings of the art-related tasks were also positive, but weaker, because unlike the writing tasks, which were all very similar, the art tasks varied considerably from one task to the next. These positive correlations showed a within-domain consistency of creativity ratings, as both domain specificity and domain generality predict, although with significantly lower correlations on different tasks, even those in the same domain. The test for domain generality came from the cross-domain correlations, of which there were 13 in all. Of those 13 correlations, some were positive, some were negative, and none—not a single one—of those 13 was statistically significant. The results were exactly what domain specificity predicted and not at all what domain generality predicted. The fact that even within the same domain the correlations were much lower when the tasks were more varied supports (a) Pretz and McCollum's (2014) argument about the need not just for domain-specific analyses, but for subdomain or task-specific analyses and (b) Barbot et al.'s (2011) suggestion that in teaching for creativity, the proper unit of analysis is the specific task.

Dow and Mayer (2004) showed the importance of such subdomain focus in their study of teaching students how to solve different kinds of insight problems. They addressed the issue of domain specificity/generality in creativity training very directly:

> The purpose of this research was to investigate whether insight problem solving depends on domain-specific or domain-general problem-solving skills, that is, whether people think in terms of conceptually different types of insight problems. (p. 389)

> Training of creative problem solving has a somewhat disappointing history, because learning to solve one kind of problem rarely supports solving of other types of problems. (p. 397)

Dow and Mayer trained their subjects in ways to solve either verbal insight problems or spatial insight problems. The training worked: subjects improved their skill in solving whichever kind of insight problems they were given. But when they compared the effects of training on skill in solving the other kind of insight problems, their results were "consistent with the domain-specific theory of insight problem solving, namely, the idea that insight problems are not a unitary general category but rather should be thought of as a collection of distinct types of problems" (p. 397). There was simply no evidence of transfer or generalization: subjects' increased ability to solve one kind of insight problem had no effect on their ability to solve other kinds of insight problems:

> What is learned when someone learns how to solve spatial insight problems? Our research suggests that students learn a general strategy that applies only to a subcategory of insight problems—that is, learning to overcome self-imposed constraints in solving spatial insight problems. (p. 391)

There is no transfer within the domain of solving different kinds of insight problems, so it should come as no surprise that there is no transfer to other kinds of creativity-relevant tasks either, including real-world creative behavior. Beaty, Nusbaum, and Silvia (2014) looked at the correlations between success at solving classic insight problems and real-world creative achievement and concluded that there was "no evidence for a relationship between insight problem solving behavior and creative behavior and achievement" (p. 287). Insight problem solving, they concluded, was unrelated to other kinds of creativity, and Dow and Mayer's (2004) study showed that even within the domain of insight problem solving, further domain specificity was called for. Creativity training can work, as all these studies demonstrate. But the success of the training is limited to the domain, or subdomain, in which the training occurs.

Does this mean that creativity training doesn't work? Not at all. But it does mean that creativity and creativity training don't operate in vacuums. They must focus on specific content. For example, Baer (1996) trained middle school students using a variety of divergent-thinking activities related to poetry-writing creativity, such as brainstorming words that could stand for other words or ideas (metaphor production) and brainstorming words with similar beginning sounds (alliteration), whereas a matched control group received unrelated training. A week later the students' regular English teachers assigned poetry- and story-writing activities without reference to the training. The students who had a week earlier received the poetry-relevant creativity training wrote poems that earned higher creativity ratings from experts than poems written by the matched control group. This training did not lead them to write more creative stories than did students in that same control group, however, even though poetry writing and story writing are from the same larger domain of writing.

Think about how students learn other kinds of things. If we want students to learn calculus, world history, and biology, we don't assume some general kind of study will help them learn all three. We understand that these are different domains, that each requires domain-specific instruction and study, and that there is little reason to expect much transfer among them. Ditto for creative-thinking skills.

Alternatively, think about other kinds of thinking skills, such as those outlined in Bloom's eponymous Taxonomy of the Cognitive Domain (Bloom, Englehart, Frost, Hill, & Krathwohl, 1956). The "higher order" skills of analysis, synthesis, and evaluation are certainly important and need to be taught, but like creative-thinking skills (which often rely on analysis, synthesis, and evaluation, as well as Bloom's other cognitive skills— knowledge, comprehension, and application), Bloom's cognitive skills also need to be taught (and learned) within the context of domains.

Consider dissection, which is a kind of analysis. Being able to dissect a frog, dissect an argument, dissect a triangle, and dissect a villanelle are all wonderful skills, but they are unrelated skills that share a generic name and little else (and the fact that a student can do any one of these tells one nothing about her ability to do any of the others). Ditto for being able to synthesize chemicals, synthesize musical sounds, synthesize columns of data, or synthesize two philosophical arguments. Cognitive skills at the level discussed by Bloom are remarkably domain- and content-specific. (Baer, in press-a)

There are simply no domain-general, decontextualized thinking skills, only domain- and content-specific thinking skills, whether those skills are the ones outlined by Bloom or the ones more frequently associated with creative thinking (Baer, 1993; Kaufman & Baer, 2005, 2006; Owen et al., 2010; Redick et al., 2013; Thompson et al., 2013; Willingham, 2007, 2008). Like expertise, and like creativity, higher level thinking skills are very domain specific.

Does this mean we can't teach creativity? Of course not. It only means that trying to use shortcuts—trying to teach creativity in a vacuum, as if content didn't matter—will be no more effective than trying to teach fractions and physics by studying something other than fractions and physics. We teach content by domain, and we need to teach thinking skills—including creative thinking skills—within the context of domains.

It isn't just the skills and knowledge needed for creativity that vary by domain. Different kinds of motivation, attitudes, and personality traits are also needed. It has been persuasively argued by Amabile and others, for example, that intrinsic motivation is conducive to creativity (Amabile, 1983, 1996; Baer, 1997, 1998a; Hennessey, 1995; Hennessey & Zbikowski, 1993). But intrinsic motivation isn't fungible across domains. One cannot cash out an interest in sports as an interest in history, and a motivation to write fiction is not readily convertible into an interest in filling out one's tax return. Similarly, there is evidence from personality testing that conscientiousness—one of the Big Five personality traits—has a significant positive impact on creativity in some domains (such as some scientific fields) and a significant negative impact in others (such as some artistic fields; Feist, 1998, 1999).

But what about interdisciplinary thinking? Does teaching with a domain-based focus ignore the power of interdisciplinary thinking? Not at all. But interdisciplinary thinking isn't simply taking what one knows (or knows how to do) and applying it in some other domain. Trying to do that without understanding the target domain is a ticket to failure. The concept of interdisciplinary thinking suggests thinking and problem solving that draw on the work of more than one discipline. It doesn't suggest that disciplines don't matter. If anything, it suggests just the opposite; without disciplines, there can be no interdisciplinary anything. "Just as creativity requires the kinds of skills and content knowledge that the Common Core is designed to promote, interdisciplinary thinking requires the kinds of expertise that disciplines develop" (Baer, in press-b).

Interdisciplinary thinking and problem solving require expertise and creative problem-solving skills in *multiple* domains. Having multiple areas of expertise and diverse domain-specific problem-solving skills may make it possible to recognize ways of solving problems that expertise and skill in only one domain would not allow. Domain specificity puts a premium on having *multiple* domain-based skills and areas of expertise. This makes it possible to solve problems in one domain that might benefit from ideas rooted in other domains as well as problems that are multidisciplinary in

NEW DIRECTIONS FOR CHILD AND ADOLESCENT DEVELOPMENT • DOI: 10.1002/cad

nature (e.g., global warming, a problem that will require expertise in many domains to solve).

So we need to teach creativity, but trying to do it in a vacuum will only invite failure. And failure in creativity training not only means time wasted (although it certainly does mean that). It also means that less time will be devoted to teaching for creativity in the future, because, based on past failures, it hardly seems worth it. The poor results teachers and administrators have observed from poorly designed creativity-training programs will unfortunately hinder future creativity-training efforts. We need to stop making the same mistakes.

We need to heed to results of research, which shows that creativity training can be very successful—if, as Barbot et al. (2011) reminded us, if it is "tailored to enhance creativity in a specific domain, and even better in a specific task" (p. 130) and "take[s] into account the multidimensionality and domain specificity of the construct of creativity" (p. 128). Doing poor creativity training poisons the well for future, better designed creativity training. We need to listen to the clear message that research that is sending us: Creativity doesn't exist, and can't be taught, in a vacuum. But if we teach it in the context of content, content that matters to us and our students, then we will not only succeed in helping our students become more creative thinkers, we will also be helping them acquire the skills and content knowledge that the standards and accountability movements value so highly. Standards (like the Common Core) are not the enemy of creativity. The two are natural allies, but we need to design programs in ways that allow them to complement each other, not ones that set them at odds.

References

Amabile, T. M. (1982). Social psychology of creativity: A consensual assessment technique. *Journal of Personality and Social Psychology, 43,* 997–1013.

Amabile, T. M. (1983). *The social psychology of creativity.* New York: Springer-Verlag.

Amabile, T. M. (1996). *Creativity in context: Update to "The Social Psychology of Creativity."* Boulder, CO: Westview.

Anastasi, A. (1982). *Psychological testing.* New York: Macmillan.

Baer, J. (1993). *Creativity and divergent thinking: A task-specific approach.* Hillsdale, NJ: Lawrence Erlbaum Associates.

Baer, J. (1994a). Divergent thinking is not a general trait: A multi-domain training experiment. *Creativity Research Journal, 7,* 35–46.

Baer, J. (1994b). Generality of creativity across performance domains: A replication. *Perceptual and Motor Skills, 79,* 1217–1218.

Baer, J. (1994c). Performance assessments of creativity: Do they have long-term stability? *Roeper Review, 7*(1), 7–11.

Baer, J. (1996). The effects of task-specific divergent-thinking training. *Journal of Creative Behavior, 30,* 183–187.

Baer, J. (1997). Gender differences in the effects of anticipated evaluation on creativity. *Creativity Research Journal, 10,* 25–31.

Baer, J. (1998a). Gender differences in the effects of extrinsic motivation on creativity. *Journal of Creative Behavior, 32,* 18–37.

Baer, J. (1998b). The case for domain specificity in creativity. *Creativity Research Journal*, *11*, 173–177.

Baer, J. (1999). Creativity in a climate of standards. *Focus on Education*, *43*, 16–21.

Baer, J. (2002). Are creativity and content standards allies or enemies? *Research in the Schools*, *9*(2), 35–42.

Baer, J. (2009, August). Are the Torrance Tests still relevant in the 21st century? Invited address, presented at the annual meeting of the American Psychological Association, Boston, MA.

Baer, J. (2010). Is creativity domain specific? In J. C. Kaufman & R. J. Sternberg (Eds.), *Cambridge handbook of creativity* (pp. 321–341). New York: Cambridge University Press.

Baer, J. (2013). Domain specificity and the limits of creativity theory. *Journal of Creative Behavior*, *46*, 16–29.

Baer, J. (2015). The importance of domain specific expertise in creativity. *Roeper Review*, *37*, 165–178. doi: 10.1080/02783193.2015.1047480

Baer, J. (2016). *Domain specificity and creativity*. San Diego, CA: Elsevier.

Baer, J. (in press-a). Content matters: Why nurturing creativity is so different in different domains. In R. A. Beghetto & B. Sriraman (Eds.), *Creative contradictions in education*. New York: Springer.

Baer, J. (in press-b). Creativity and the Common Core need each other. In D. Ambrose & R. J. Sternberg (Eds.), *Creative intelligence in the 21st century: Grappling with enormous problems and huge opportunities*. Rotterdam, Netherlands: Sense Publishers.

Baer, J., & Kaufman, J. C. (2012). *Being creative inside and outside the classroom*. Rotterdam: Sense Publishers.

Baer, J., Kaufman, J. C., & Gentile, C. A. (2004). Extension of the consensual assessment technique to nonparallel creative products. *Creativity Research Journal*, *16*, 113–117.

Barbot, B., Besançon, M., & Lubart, T. I. (2011). Assessing creativity in the classroom. *Open Education Journal*, *4*(Suppl. 2, M5), 124–132.

Beaty, R. E., Nusbaum, E. C., & Silvia, P. J. (2014). Does insight problem solving predict real-world creativity? *Psychology of Aesthetics, Creativity, and the Arts*, *8*(3), 287.

Beghetto, R. A. (2013). *Killing ideas softly?: The promise and perils of creativity in the classroom*. Charlotte, NC: Information Age Publishing.

Beghetto, R., Kaufman, J., & Baer, J. (2015). *Teaching for creativity in the Common Core classroom*. New York: Teachers College Press.

Besançon, M., Lubart, T., & Barbot, B. (2013). Creative giftedness and educational opportunities. *Educational & Child Psychology*, *30*(2), 161–171.

Bloom, B. S., Engelhart, M. D., Furst, F. J., Hill, W. H., & Krathwohl, D. R. (1956). *Handbook I: cognitive domain. Taxonomy of educational objectives: The classification of education goals*. New York: Longman.

Conti, R., Coon, H., & Amabile, T. M. (1996). Evidence to support the componential model of creativity: Secondary analyses of three studies. *Creativity Research Journal*, *9*, 385–389.

Crockenberg, S. B. (1972). Creativity tests: A boon or boondoggle for education? *Review of Educational Research*, *42*, 27–45.

Csikszentmihalyi, M. (1988). Society, culture, and person: A systems view of creativity. In R. J. Sternberg (Ed.), *The nature of creativity: Contemporary psychological perspectives* (pp. 325–339). New York: Cambridge University Press.

Csikszentmihalyi, M. (2013). *Creativity: The psychology of discovery and invention*. New York: HarperCollins.

Dow, G. T., & Mayer, R. E. (2004). Teaching students to solve insight problems: Evidence for domain specificity in creativity training. *Creativity Research Journal*, *16*(4), 389–398.

Feist, G. J. (1998). A meta-analysis of personality in scientific and artistic creativity. *Personality and Social Psychology Review, 2*(4), 290–309.

Feist, G. J. (1999). The influence of personality on artistic and scientific creativity. In R. J. Sternberg (Ed.), *Handbook of creativity* (pp. 273–296). New York: Cambridge University Press.

Gardner, H. (1993). *Creating minds.* New York: Basic Books.

Hennessey, B. A. (1995). Social, environmental, and developmental issues and creativity. *Educational Psychology Review, 7*(2), 163–183.

Hennessey, B. A., & Zbikowski, S. M. (1993). Immunizing children against the negative effects of reward: A further examination of intrinsic motivation training techniques. *Creativity Research Journal, 6*(3), 297–307.

Ivcevic, Z. (2007). Artistic and everyday creativity: An act-frequency approach. *Journal of Creative Behavior, 41,* 271–290.

Kaufman, J. C., & Baer, J. (Eds.). (2005). *Creativity across domains: Faces of the muse.* Hillsdale, NJ: Lawrence Erlbaum Associates.

Kaufman, J. C., & Baer, J. (Eds.). (2006). *Reason and creativity in development.* Cambridge University Press.

Kim, K. H. (2009, August). Are the Torrance Tests still relevant in the 21st century? Invited address, presented at the annual meeting of the American Psychological Association, Boston, MA.

Owen, A. M., Hampshire, A., Grahn, J. A., Stenton, R., Dajani, S., Burns, A. S., Howard, R. G., & Ballard, C. G. (2010). Putting brain training to the test. *Nature, 465*(7299), 775–778

Plucker, J. A. (1998). Beware of simple conclusions: The case for the content generality of creativity. *Creativity Research Journal, 11,* 179–182.

Plucker, J. A., & Beghetto, R. A. (2015). Introduction to the special issue. *Psychology of Aesthetics, Creativity, and the Arts, 9*(2), 115.

Pretz, J. E., & McCollum, V. A. (2014). Self-perceptions of creativity do not always reflect actual creative performance. *Psychology of Aesthetics, Creativity, and the Arts, 8,* 227.

Redick, T. S., Shipstead, Z., Harrison, T. L., Hicks, K. L., Fried, D. E., Hambrick, D. Z., Kane, M. J., & Engle, R. W. (2013). No evidence of intelligence improvement after working memory training: a randomized, placebo-controlled study. *Journal of Experimental Psychology: General, 142*(2), 359.

Runco, M. A. (1989). The creativity of children's art. *Child Study Journal, 19,* 177–190.

Sawyer, K. (2012). *Explaining creativity: The science of human innovation* (2nd ed.). New York: Oxford University Press.

Scott, G., Leritz, L. E., & Mumford, M. D. (2004). The effectiveness of creativity training: A quantitative review. *Creativity Research Journal, 16*(4), 361–388.

Sternberg, R. J. (1985). Implicit theories of intelligence, creativity, and wisdom. *Journal of Personality and Social Psychology, 49,* 607–627.

Sternberg, R. J. (2015). Teaching for creativity: The sounds of silence. *Psychology of Aesthetics, Creativity, and the Arts, 9*(2), 115–117.

Sternberg, R. J., & Lubart, T. I. (1995). *Defying the crowd. Cultivating creativity in a culture of conformity.* New York: Free Press.

Thompson, T. W., Waskom, M. L., Garel, K. L. A., Cardenas-Iniguez, C., Reynolds, G. O., Winter, R., Chang, P., Pollard, K., Lala, N., Alvarez, G. A., & Gabrieli, J. D. E. (2013). Failure of working memory training to enhance cognition or intelligence. *PloS one, 8*(5), e63614. Retrieved online January 10, 2014, at http://www.plosone.org/article/info%3Adoi%2F10.1371%2Fjournal.pone.0063614.

Torrance, E. P. (1972a). Career patterns and peak creative achievements of creative high school students twelve years later. *Gifted Child Quarterly, 16,* 75–88.

Torrance, E. P. (1972b). Predictive validity of the Torrance Tests of Creative Thinking. *Journal of Creative Behavior, 6,* 236–252.

Willingham, D. T. (2004). Reframing the mind. *Education Next* (Summer, 2004). Retrieved February 13, 2014 at http://educationnext.org/reframing-the-mind/.

Willingham, D. (2007). Critical thinking: Why is it so hard to teach? *American Educator.* Retrieved February 13, 2014 at http://www.aft.org/newspubs/periodicals/ae/summer2007/index.cfm.

JOHN BAER *is a professor of educational psychology at Rider University. He earned his BA from Yale University and his PhD in cognitive and developmental psychology from Rutgers University.*

NEW DIRECTIONS FOR CHILD AND ADOLESCENT DEVELOPMENT • DOI: 10.1002/cad

Russ, S. W. (2016). Pretend play: Antecedent of adult creativity. In B. Barbot (Ed.), *Perspectives on creativity development. New Directions for Child and Adolescent Development, 151*, 21–32.

2

Pretend Play: Antecedent of Adult Creativity

Sandra W. Russ

Abstract

This article reviews the theoretical and empirical literature in the area of pretend play as a predictor of adult creativity. There is strong evidence that processes expressed in pretend play are associated with measures of creativity, especially with divergent thinking. There is some evidence from longitudinal studies that this association is stable over time. Converging evidence suggests that cognitive and affective processes in pretend play are involved in adult creative production. However, there is a lack of consensus in the field as to whether engaging in pretend play actually facilitates creative thinking. In addition, many other variables (opportunity, tolerance for failure, motivation, work ethic, etc.) determine whether children with creative potential are actually creative in adulthood. In spite of the many methodological challenges in conducting research in the play area, it is important to continue investigating specific processes expressed in play and their developmental trajectories. Large samples in multisite studies would be ideal in investigating the ability of specific play processes to predict these creative processes and creative productivity in adulthood. © 2016 Wiley Periodicals, Inc.

NEW DIRECTIONS FOR CHILD AND ADOLESCENT DEVELOPMENT, no. 151, Spring 2016 © 2016 Wiley Periodicals, Inc.
Published online in Wiley Online Library (wileyonlinelibrary.com). • DOI: 10.1002/cad.20154

Creativity scholars have often speculated that pretend play abilities in childhood are associated with creative production in adulthood. Similar cognitive and affective processes occur in both pretend play and creative production. A creative product is one that is original, of good quality, and appropriate to the task (Sternberg, Kaufman, & Pretz, 2002). Creative processes that occur within the individual are involved in development of a creative product. Research has found that cognitive processes that are important in creative production include divergent thinking, broad associative ability, flexibility of thought, insight, and analogical thinking (Guilford, 1950; Runco, 2004; Sawyer, 2012). To invent a new creative product, be it a musical composition, piece of fiction, or scientific theory, one must have a knowledge base but then engage in divergent thinking (generate a variety of ideas), search one's memory broadly, think flexibly, and break out of current theoretical frames or problem-solving approaches. Individuals who are high in these cognitive abilities should better be able to produce a creative work of art or scientific invention.

More recently, affective processes are being recognized as important in creative production (Bass, De Dreu, & Nijstad, 2008; Isen, Daubman, & Nowicki, 1987; Russ, 1993). The ability to think about ideas and images that involve emotion have been related to creativity in adults (Suler, 1980) and children (Russ, 1982; Russ & Grossman-McKee, 1990). Individuals who can think about affect-laden ideas and images and express these affect themes do better on measures of creativity than those who are more restricted in their thinking. The ability to experience emotion, especially positive emotion, has been found to increase creative cognitive abilities in a number of studies (Bass et al., 2008). Also, the capacity to experience joy in creative expression is a key component of intrinsic motivation (Amabile, 1983). The love of the work is important in creative production.

What does this research literature have to do with children's pretend play? Pretend play is where these creative cognitive and affective processes occur, are practiced, and can be measured.

What Happens in Pretend Play?

Pretend play is a vehicle for the expression of many processes that are important in creative production. Pretend play is symbolic behavior in which "one thing is playfully treated as if it were something else" (Fein, 1987, p. 282). Krasnor and Pepler (1980) conceptualized play as involving nonliterality, positive affect, intrinsic motivation, and flexibility. They viewed play as reflecting the developmental level of the child and also as providing the child with an opportunity to practice skills. They also thought play was a causal agent in developmental change.

In pretend play, children use objects to represent other objects (a stick is a sword), make up stories, use fantasy, role-play, and express affect and affect themes (i.e., war, eating, monsters, illness, fun games). Russ (2014)

Table 2.1. Model of Creativity and Pretend Play

Creative Processes in Pretend Play	Examples in Play
Divergent thinking	Block transformations
Broad associations	Different story ideas and elements
	Wide fantasy and remote images
Cognitive flexibility/recombining ideas	Use of toys in different ways
	Manipulation of story elements
	Loosening of time and space
Insight and problem solving	Building novel objects
	Playing with mechanical objects
Perspective-taking	Role playing
	Pretending to be different characters
Narrative development	Story plots and sequences
Affect themes and symbols	Monsters; cops and robbers
	Yummy food
Emotional expression	Dolls fighting; dolls hugging
Joy in pretending	Pleasure and absorption in the play
Integration of affect/affect themes	Placing emotion in an appropriate narrative

Source: Russ, S. (2014). Pretend play in childhood: Foundation of adult creativity. Washington, DC: American Psychological Association (p. 25).

reviewed that cognitive and affective processes are important in both pretend play and creativity (see Table 2.1). Cognitive processes include divergent thinking (generating a variety of ideas), symbolism, organization of a story; fantasy/make-believe, and recombining of objects, images, and memories. Affective processes include affect-laden themes and symbols, emotional expression, joy in playing, and integration of affect themes into cognition. A boy who has a puppet use blocks as a telescope to see the moon and then rides the blocks as a rocket ship to get to the moon is transforming the blocks into different objects, demonstrating divergent thinking and symbolism. This boy is also using fantasy and organizing a story. A girl who has two puppets go to a birthday party and eat cake that is "really yummy" (blocks are the table and a lego is the cake) and jumps up and down and laughs when they win a prize after a race is transforming the blocks, making a story, expressing affect themes (good cake, winning a race), and expressing emotion (puppets laughing).

When children are playing, they are making things up. This kind of thinking is self-generated thought. Self-generated thought is a term in neuroscience to describe a type of thought important in creative thinking (Jauk, Benedek, & Neubauer, 2015). Children call on memories, television shows, daily life, or books to develop their stories. But they are choosing what content to use and how to recombine their memories and thoughts. Singer and Singer (1990) proposed that pretend play was practice with divergent thinking. We can expand that concept to practice with a variety of forms of cognitive and affective abilities that are involved in creativity.

There are a number of theoretical explanations for the relationship between pretend play and creativity (see Russ, 2014, and Russ & Wallace, 2013, for reviews). Theoretically, Vygotsky (1930/1967) thought that imagination developed from children's play and that creativity itself was a developmental process. He thought that pretend play was a creative reworking of past experience that meets the needs of the child (p. 7). Dansky (1980) and Kogan (1983) focused on the free combination of ideas and objects that occur in play as important in creative thinking. Fein (1987) thought that both affect and cognition were intertwined in pretend play and that affect symbols were being manipulated. She proposed an affect symbol system composed of symbolic units that represented affective relationships such as fear of, love of, anger at, etc. that involved real or imagined emotional experiences. These units are "manipulated, interpreted, coordinated and elaborated in a way that makes affective sense to the players" (p. 292). These affect-laden themes and cognitions should provide a richer store of associations and memories that the individual child (or adult) can call upon when creating. Isen et al. (1987) hypothesized that the reason positive affect increases creativity is because it primes and broadens the association process. Broad associations increase the odds of remote associations that are original. The concept of playfulness also involves positive affect during the play session itself. Singer and Singer (1990) have stressed that play helps children express and regulate emotions, positive and negative, so that they have the capacity to feel, express, and think about emotion. Negative affect themes (aggression, sadness, fear) are also important in pretend play. Psychoanalytic theory proposed that not being able to think about conflict-laden content or content that was taboo would result in a general intellectual restriction. In other words, repression would interfere with the creative process (Freud, 1926/1959). Kris (1952) built upon this concept and hypothesized that individuals who could easily access primary process thoughts (sexual and aggressive, and illogical ideation) and also call upon logical thinking, would be more creative.

Finally, the fun, and sometimes joy, that children experience when playing is very rewarding and could foster a desire to experience this kind of feeling again. The "flow" and deep engagement that many children experience in pretend play is an example of the "flow" experience defined by Csikszentmihalyi (1990) in creative production. Play could set the stage for wanting to engage in creative activities and experience the joy of creation.

Creative adults often report on the importance of pretend play in their development. Root-Bernstein and Root-Bernstein (2006) studied imaginary worlds (paracosms) in MacArthur "genius" fellows and college students. They found that 26% of MacArthur fellows reported having imaginary worlds in childhood compared with 12% of college students. Other creative artists and scientists describe the importance of pretend play in their childhood and describe processes in their creativity that are similar to processes expressed in pretend play (Russ, 2014).

Empirical Evidence

What about empirical support for the association between processes in pretend play and creativity? Is the association stable over time? Is there evidence for a causal relationship between pretend play and creativity? The idea that pretend play provides an opportunity for practicing with different cognitive and affective processes implies that play facilitates these abilities.

There are a number of methodological challenges in studying pretend play, many of which have been enumerated by Lillard et al. (2013). Studies often lack control groups, have unblinded researchers, lack random assignment, and have small sample sizes. In addition, different measures of play are used in different studies and studies are often global in nature rather than focusing on specific processes. It is not pretend play that should be the focus; it is the specific processes reflected in the play expressions that need to be measured and manipulated (Russ & Wallace, 2013).

There are a variety of pretend play measures that have been used in research. Most have been developed for particular studies in different research programs. (See Gitlin-Weiner, Sandgrund, and Schaefer, 2000, and Kaugars, 2011, for reviews of pretend play measures.) Also, most play measures have focused on cognitive processes. Rubin, Fein, and Vandenberg (1983) referred to this phenomenon as the "cognification" of play. Russ developed the Affect in Play Scale (APS, 1993, 2004) to measure both cognitive and affective processes in play in 6- to 10-year-olds. The APS measures imagination and organization of the narrative on a 1–5 scale. It also measures affect themes and expression of emotion in the narrative with a frequency count. Finally, it measures enjoyment of and absorption in the play task. These are processes that are also important in creativity. The APS is a 5-minute play task using puppets and blocks that asks the child to have the puppets do something together. There is a version of the task for younger children (APS-P) that uses a variety of toys with more structured instructions for 4- and 5-year-olds. APS has been found to relate to divergent thinking in five different studies with different school-aged child populations, independent of verbal intelligence (Hoffmann & Russ, 2012; Russ & Grossman-McKee, 1990; Russ & Schafer, 2006; Russ, Robins, & Christiano, 1999, Wallace & Russ, 2015). The consistent finding that these play processes are associated with divergent thinking when verbal intelligence is controlled for is important and suggests that these abilities are separate from general intelligence. The preschool version, the APS-P, related to divergent thinking in two studies (Fehr & Russ, in press; Kaugars & Russ, 2009).

Most of the research on play and creativity in the literature has focused on play and divergent thinking. Some of the reasons for this are that divergent thinking is thought to be important in creativity, is relatively easy to assess in children, and has measures available that are valid. There is some criticism of divergent thinking as a measure of creativity. Kaufman, Plucker, and Baer (2008) concluded that divergent thinking tests do not predict creative ability in many studies. However, there is strong evidence of predictive validity of the Torrance Test of Creative Thinking (Kim, 2008). A 40-year follow-up of that divergent thinking test found that it predicted creative achievement 40 years later (Cramond, Mathews-Morgan, Bandalos, & Zuo, 2005) and also 50 years later (Runco, Millar, Acar, & Cramond, 2011). These follow-up studies provide stronger empirical support that divergent thinking ability in childhood is predictive of creative functioning in adulthood. Tests of divergent thinking continue to be widely used in the child creativity area.

Correlational Studies

A large number of studies have found significant relationships between different measures of pretend play and divergent thinking. (See Dansky, 1999, and Russ, 2014, for reviews.) Some of these studies have been criticized in the recent review by Lillard et al. (2013) for having the same individual administer the play task and the divergent thinking task, which raises the possibility of experimenter bias. However, there are studies that did use different examiners and found significant associations, as hypothesized, between the play measure and divergent thinking (Lieberman, 1977; Russ & Grossman-McKee, 1990; Russ et al., 1999; Singer & Rummo, 1973, Wallace & Russ, 2015).

Studies have also found relationships between play and other measures of creativity. Kaugars and Russ (2009) found that pretend play in preschool children on the APS-P related to teacher ratings of make-believe in children's daily play behavior. Hoffmann and Russ (2012) found that pretend play related to creativity in storytelling, independent of verbal ability. The stories were rated for creativity by independent raters. Given the number of studies in the literature in different research programs, with different child populations, and in different environments that have found significant relations between pretend play and creativity, with some studies using different examiners for the different tasks, Russ and Wallace (2013) concluded that there is good evidence for the association between pretend play and creativity.

In most of the studies with the APS, both cognitive (imagination and organization) and affect (frequency and variety of affect themes) in fantasy play related to the creativity measures. This is important because affect has been neglected in the play research area and yet is so important in creativity. The amount of affect expressed in play, both positive and negative affect, related to divergent thinking.

Longitudinal Studies

Theoretically, pretend play should be predictive of creativity over time. Guilford (1950) expected that creative processes would be stable. Developmental theory would expect stability of individual differences in cognition and affect. A few longitudinal studies support this expectation.

NEW DIRECTIONS FOR CHILD AND ADOLESCENT DEVELOPMENT • DOI: 10.1002/cad

Hutt and Bhavnani (1972) found that inventiveness in preschool play related to later divergent thinking. Shmukler (1982–1983) found that preschool imaginative disposition and expressive imagination in play related to later imagination. Clark, Griffing, and Johnson (1989) also found that play in preschoolers was predictive of divergent thinking over a 3-year period. Mullineaux and Dilalla (2009) found that preschool realistic role-play involving pretending at age 5 was predictive of divergent thinking on the Alternate Uses Measure when the children were 10–15 years old.

There have been two longitudinal studies carried out with the APS. The first was a longitudinal study by Russ et al. (1999) that found that imagination in early play predicted divergent thinking 4 years later (r = .42, p < .01). In that study, measures of creativity of stories and creative activities were also obtained. For the most part, early play did not predict these other measures of creativity. Interestingly, the measures of creativity did not relate to one another. Those children were followed into high school, and results were that quality of fantasy in early play continued to predict divergent thinking in the 11th and 12th grades (r = .28, p < .05, Russ & Cooperberg, 2002).

In a recent longitudinal study that followed the children in the Hoffmann and Russ (2012) study, Wallace and Russ (2015) found that pretend play predicted divergent thinking in girls over a 4-year period. For example, after verbal intelligence was controlled, imagination in early play was related to divergent thinking fluency (r = .39, p < .01), as was organization of the narrative (r = .51, p < .01). Positive affect in play was associated with originality (r = .36, p < .05). These results replicated the Russ et al. (1999) findings. In addition, when baseline divergent thinking was controlled for, play continued to significantly predict divergent thinking. This suggests that components of play in addition to divergent thinking are associated with shifts in divergent thinking over time. Children whose early pretend play was imaginative, with a well-organized narrative, were better divergent thinkers 4 years later, independent of baseline divergent thinking ability. Pretend play also predicted math computation achievement, perhaps because of the cognitive flexibility involved in manipulating symbols. These girls will be followed into high school and creative functioning will be assessed.

Longitudinal research is difficult to carry out. One has to plan ahead and find appropriate incentives for children and parents to participate. This is a challenge during the adolescent years especially. And, in the area of creativity, there are so many variables that determine whether the creative potential that is evident in pretend play or divergent thinking is acted on in adulthood (Runco, 2004). Whether or not an individual actually produces a creative product depends upon opportunity, talent, work ethic, tolerance for failure, risk taking, motivation, openness to experience, etc., in addition to creative cognitive and affective processes within the individual. Because there are so many variables involved in determining creative output, it is

NEW DIRECTIONS FOR CHILD AND ADOLESCENT DEVELOPMENT • DOI: 10.1002/cad

difficult for definitive longitudinal studies to predict actual creative production. Pretend play may predict divergent thinking in adolescents, but whether these adolescents use this divergent thinking ability in creative activities is dependent on many other personality variables, interests, and opportunities. It is probably more realistic for longitudinal studies in the play area to stay focused on the cognitive and affective processes in play, and to assess their stability over time, and into adulthood. This is consistent with Plucker, Runco, and Lim's (2006) conclusion that the criteria in creativity prediction studies should not be removed too far from the components of the predictor. For example, does the child with a high frequency of affect in play have a high frequency of affect in memories and stories as an adult? In two cross-sectional studies, affect in play does relate to affect in memories (Russ & Schafer, 2006) and affect in stories (Hoffmann & Russ, 2012). If this association remains stable into adulthood, then these affective processes could be used in creative production.

Experimental Studies

What about the evidence for pretend play as a facilitator of creativity? There is controversy in the literature as to whether there is any evidence that pretend play facilitates creativity. Lillard et al. (2013) concluded that there is no support for play having a causal effect on creativity. They conclude that there are major methodological problems with the studies in the literature and that there is a lack of replication. On the other hand, Dansky (1999) and Russ (2014) concluded that there are well-done studies with adequate controls that have found that engaging in pretend play or play training sessions have facilitated imagination in play and creativity on creativity tasks.

Christie (1994) has cautioned against brief one-trial studies in the play intervention area. It may take time for the development of processes in pretend play that would, in turn, affect other tasks, such as creativity tasks. There is evidence that when pretend play occurs in multiple sessions over time, increases in components of creativity occur. For example, Kasari, Freeman, and Paparella (2006), in a randomized controlled study with children with autism, found that a play intervention resulted in increased symbolic play. These were young children from 3 to 4 years of age in a rigorous study that began the intervention at the child's current developmental level. Children in the play group, compared with children in joint attention and control groups, had increased symbolic play that generalized to play with mothers. Moore and Russ (2008) found that five sessions of play facilitation sessions resulted in increased imagination in play 4 to 8 months later. Immediately after the play sessions, there was a significant group effect in that the play group significantly increased in divergent thinking, compared with a control group. This transfer to the divergent thinking task did not remain in the follow-up study. Hoffmann and Russ (in press) found that play facilitation sessions in small groups resulted in increased imagination and affect expression in play in first- and second-grade girls when compared to a control group. For below-average players, the play training did result in significant improvement on a divergent thinking task. These results are promising and suggest that future research in this area should be pursued.

Future Directions

The reality is that research on play and creativity is very difficult to carry out in a rigorous fashion. Because this research is so labor intensive, small samples are a problem in the research literature. To obtain large samples, the field needs funding and coordinated multisite studies. Nevertheless, there is growing evidence that cognitive and affective processes in pretend play are related to measures of creative processes in children. These findings are consistent with theory and with the creativity research literature. We can measure and observe these creative processes in pretend play. One implication of these findings is that pretend play could be used to assess creative potential for gifted and talented educational programs. Pretend play assessment could add value to traditional measures for assessing creative potential.

Rigorous experimental studies of the effect of play training sessions on cognitive and affective processes and transfer effects on creativity measures need to be conducted. If children can develop these processes through pretend play, then they can increase their creative potential that, it is hoped, will be used in the future.

As a field, we should continue to investigate (a) what specific affective and cognitive processes in pretend play are related to different types of creative thinking, (b) whether these associations are stable into adulthood, and (c) how to help children develop these processes. These processes are the internal ingredients that increase the odds that, in adulthood, they will be used in creative production. There is growing evidence that these processes in pretend play are relatively stable over time and the associations between pretend play and creative thinking remain stable. Large samples in multisite studies are necessary to understand which specific processes that occur in play are associated with which domains of creative production. However, whether creative production occurs is dependent upon many variables, including parents' and teachers' reactions to creative thinking. As a society facing many serious challenges that need creative individuals, we should support longitudinal research and experimental studies that investigate these important and complex questions.

References

Amabile, T. (1983). *The social psychology of creativity*. New York: Springer-Verlag.

Bass, M., DeDreu, C.K.W., Nijstad, B.A. (2008). A meta-analysis of 25 years of mood-creativity research: Hedonic tone, activation, or regulatory focus? *Psychological Bulletin, 134*, 779–806.

NEW DIRECTIONS FOR CHILD AND ADOLESCENT DEVELOPMENT • DOI: 10.1002/cad

Christie, J. (1994). Academic play. In J. Hellendoorn, R. Van der Kooij, & B. Sutton-Smith (Eds.), *Play and intervention.* (pp. 203–213) Albany: State University of New York Press.

Clark, P., Griffing, P., & Johnson, L. (1989). Symbolic play and ideational fluency as aspects of the evolving divergent cognitive style in young children. *Early Child Development and Care, 51,* 77–88.

Cramond, B., Mathews-Morgan, J., Bandalos, D., & Zuo, L. (2005). A report on the 40-year follow-up of the Torrance Tests of Creative Thinking: Alive and well in the new millennium. *Gifted Child Quarterly, 49,* 283–291.

Csikszentmihalyi, M. (1990). *Flow: The psychology of optimal experience.* New York: Harper & Row.

Dansky, J. (1980). Make-believe: A mediator of the relationship between play and associative fluency. *Child Development, 51,* 576–579.

Dansky, J. (1999). Play. In M. Runco & S. Pritzker (Eds.), *Encyclopedia of creativity* (pp. 393–408). San Diego: Academic Press.

Fehr, K., & Russ, S. (in press). Pretend play in preschool-age children: Association and brief intervention. Psychology of Aesthetics, Creativity, and the Arts.

Fein, G. (1987). Pretend play: Creativity and consciousness. In P. Gorlitz & J. Wohlwill (Eds.), *Curiosity, imagination and play* (pp. 281–304). Hillsdale, NJ: Lawrence Erlbaum Associates.

Freud, S. (1959). Inhibition, symptoms, and anxiety. In J. Strachey (Ed. and Trans.), *The standard edition of the complete works of Sigmund Freud* (Vol. 20, pp. 87–172). London: Hogarth Press. (Original work published 1926)

Gitlin-Weiner, K., Sandgrund, A., & Schaefer, C. (2000). *Play diagnosis and assessment* (2nd ed.). New York: Wiley.

Guilford, J. P. (1950). Creativity. *American Psychologist, 5,* 444–454.

Hoffmann, J., & Russ, S. (2012). Pretend play, creativity and emotion regulation in children. *Psychology of Aesthetics, Creativity and the Arts, 6,* 175–184.

Hoffmann, J., & Russ, S. (in press). Fostering pretend play skills and creativity in elementary school girls. *Psychology of Aesthetics, Creativity and the Arts.*

Hutt, C., & Bhavnani, R. (1972). Predictions for play. *Nature, 237,* 171–172.

Isen, A., & Daubman, K., & Nowicki, G. (1987). Positive affect facilitates creative problem solving. *Journal of Personality and Social Psychology, 52,* 1122–1131.

Jauk, E., Benedek, M., & Neubauer, A. (2015, August). *Neuronal correlates of internal attention in convergent and divergent thinking.* Paper presented at American Psychological Association, Toronto.

Kasari, C., Freeman, S., & Paparella, T. (2006). Joint attention and symbolic play in young children with autism: A randomized controlled intervention study. *Journal of Child Psychology and Psychiatry, 47,* 611–620.

Kaufman, J., Plucker, J. & Baer, J. (2008). *Essentials of creativity assessment.* New York: Wiley.

Kaugars, A. (2011). Assessment of pretend play. In S. Russ & L. Niec (Eds.), *Play in clinical practice: Evidence-based approaches* (pp. 51–82). New York: Guilford Press.

Kaugars, A. S., & Russ, S. W. (2009). Assessing preschool children's pretend play: preliminary validation of the affect in play scale—preschool version. *Early Education and Development, 20,* 733–755.

Kim, K. H. (2008). Meta-analysis of the relationship of creative achievement to both IQ and divergent thinking test scores. *Journal of Creative Behavior, 42,* 106–130.

Kogan, N. (1983). Stylistic variation in childhood and adolescence: Creativity, metaphor, and cognitive styles. In P. Mussen (Ed.), *Handbook of child psychology* (Vol. 3, (pp. 631–706). New York: Wiley.

Krasnor, I., & Pepler, D. (1980). The study of children's play: Some suggested future directions. *Child Development, 9,* 85–94.

Kris, E. (1952). *Psychoanalytic explorations in art*. New York: International Universities Press.

Lieberman, J. N. (1977). *Playfulness: Its relationship to imagination and creativity*. New York: Academic Press.

Lillard, A., Lerner, M., Hopkins, E., Dore, R., Smith, E., & Palmquist, C. (2013). The impact of pretend play on children's development: A review of empirical evidence. *Psychological Bulletin, 139*, 1–34.

Mullineaux, P., & Dilalla, L.(2009). Preschool pretend play behaviors and early adolescent creativity. *Journal of Creative Behavior, 43*, 41–57.

Moore, M., & Russ, S. (2008). Follow-up of a pretend play intervention: Effects on play, creativity, and emotional processes in children. *Creativity Research Journal, 20*, 427–436.

Plucker, J., Runco, M., & Lim, W. (2006). Predicting ideational behavior from divergent thinking and discretionary time on task. *Creativity Research Journal, 18*, 55–63.

Root-Bernstein, M., & Root-Bernstein, R. (2006). Imaginary worldplay in childhood and maturity and its impact on adult creativity. *Creativity Research Journal, 18*, 405–425.

Rubin, K., Fein, G., & Vandenberg, B, (1983). Play. In P. Mussen (Ed.), *Handbook of child psychology* (Vol. 4, pp. 693–774). New York: Wiley.

Runco, M. (2004). Everyone has creative potential. In R. J. Sternberg, E. L. Grigorenko, & J. L. Singer (Eds.), *Creativity: From potential to realization* (pp. 21–30). Washington, DC: American Psychological Association.

Runco, M,. Millar, G., Acar, S., & Cramond, B. (2011). Torrance tests of creative thinking as predictors of personal and public achievement: A fifty year follow-up. *Creativity Research Journal, 22*, 361–368.

Russ, S. (1982). Sex differences in primary process thinking and flexibility in problem solving in children. *Journal of Personality Assessment, 46*, 569–577.

Russ, S. (1993). *Affect and creativity: The role of affect and play in the creative process*. Hillsdale, NJ: Lawrence Erlbaum Associates.

Russ, S. W. (2004). *Play in child development and psychotherapy: Toward empirically supported practice*. Mahwah, NJ: Lawrence Erlbaum Associates

Russ, S. (2014). *Pretend play in childhood: Foundation of adult creativity*. Washington, DC: American Psychological Association.

Russ, S.W., & Cooperberg, M. (2002). Play as a predictor of creativity, coping, and depression in adolescents. Unpublished manuscript, Department of Psychology, Case Western Reserve University, Cleveland, OH.

Russ, S. W., & Grossman-McKee, A. (1990). Affective expression in children's fantasy play, primary process thinking on the Rorschach and divergent thinking. *Journal of Personality Assessment, 54*, 756–771.

Russ, S. W., Robins, A., & Christiano, B. (1999). Pretend play: longitudinal prediction of creativity and affect in fantasy in children. *Creativity Research Journal, 12*, 129–139.

Russ, S. W., & Schafer, E. (2006). Affect in fantasy play, emotion in memories and divergent thinking. *Creativity Research Journal, 18*, 347–354.

Russ, S., & Wallace, C. (2013). Pretend play and creative processes. *American Journal of Play, 6*, 136–148.

Sawyer, K. (2012). *Explaining creativity* (2nd ed.). New York: Oxford University Press.

Shmukler, D. (1982–1983). Early home background features in relation to imagination and creative expression in third grade. *Imagination, Cognition, and Personality, 2*, 311–321.

Singer, D. L., & Rummo, J. (1973). Ideational creativity and behavioral style in kindergarten-age children. *Developmental Psychology, 8*, 154–161.

Singer, D. G., & Singer, J. L. (1990). *The house of make-believe: Children's play and the developing imagination*. Cambridge, MA: Harvard University Press.

Sternberg, R. J., Kaufman, J. C., & Pretz, J. E. (2002). *The creativity conundrum*. New York: Psychology Press.

Suler, J. (1980). Primary process thinking and creativity. *Psychological Bulletin, 88*, 144–165.

Vygotsky, L. S. (1967). *Vaobraszeniye i tvorchestvov deskom voraste* [Imagination and creativity in childhood]. Moscow: Prosvescheniye. (Original work published 1930).

Wallace, C., & Russ, S. (2015). Pretend play, divergent thinking, and achievement in girls: A longitudinal study. *Psychology of Aesthetics, Creativity and the Arts, 9*, 296–305.

SANDRA W. RUSS is Distinguished University Professor and Louis D. Beaumont University Professor, Department of Psychological Sciences, Case Western Reserve University.

Barbot, B., Lubart, T. I. & Besançon, M. (2016). "Peaks, slumps, and bumps": Individual differences in the development of creativity in children and adolescents. In B. Barbot (Ed.), *Perspectives on creativity development. New Directions for Child and Adolescent Development, 151,* 33–45.

3

"Peaks, Slumps, and Bumps": Individual Differences in the Development of Creativity in Children and Adolescents

Baptiste Barbot, Todd I. Lubart, Maud Besançon

Abstract

This article reviews developmental studies of creativity in children and adolescents with a focus on "peaks" and "slumps" that have often been described in the literature. The irregularity of the development of creativity is interpreted in light of conceptual and measurement issues and with regard to the interaction between individual-level resources, task-specific demands, and environmental influences, resulting in apparent individual differences in the development of creativity. The need for longitudinal designs, multidimensional and multi-domain assessment of creative potential limiting the contribution of task-specific factors is outlined and discussed as an important direction for developmental research on creativity. © 2016 Wiley Periodicals, Inc.

NEW DIRECTIONS FOR CHILD AND ADOLESCENT DEVELOPMENT, no. 151, Spring 2016 © 2016 Wiley Periodicals, Inc.
Published online in Wiley Online Library (wileyonlinelibrary.com). • DOI: 10.1002/cad.20152

"Peaks," "slumps," and "bumps": there are not enough terms to describe the discontinuity in the development of creativity throughout the life span. Illustrated by the lives of eminent creators, "a work that brings its creator unprecedented acclaim may be followed by an embarrassing fiasco" (Simonton, 2000, p. 312). What are the common developmental trends in the development of creativity and why are there differences in these trends across cultures, school environments, and people? Why do some children experience a creativity slump and others do not? Why do some children never "recover" from a creativity slump?

After presenting a general framework on creative potential and conceptual distinctions with creative achievement, this article addresses these questions by reviewing classic and recent developmental studies of creativity in children and adolescents, with a focus on patterns of discontinuity. We outline multiple explanatory causes of these patterns and discuss methodological issues of studies showing these trends. Finally, we present a model of the development of creativity that explains individual differences in light of the interaction between individual-level resources, environmental influences, and task-specific demands. We conclude by discussing important areas of focus for the field's research agenda.

Nature of Creativity and Creative Potential

Creativity is the ability to produce original work that fits within particular task or domain constraints (e.g., Sternberg & Lubart, 1995). Consistent with this classic definition, which emphasizes the concept of "an ability" (rather than a set of "abilities"), it is often thought that creativity represents a generalized or unitary entity ("*g-factor view*"), despite evidence for its multidimensionality and domain specificity reported for decades (e.g., Baer, 1998; Wallach, 1970). This *g-factor view*, however, leads to misconceptions about the nature of creativity and its development (Barbot, Besançon, & Lubart, 2015). In this regard, it is important to distinguish between creative achievement and creative potential, as each could follow fairly distinct developmental pathways.

Creative achievement refers to an accomplished creative output, recognized as valuable in a domain-based context. This output may be seen on a unidimensional continuum ranging from low to outstanding creativity depending on its level of originality and appropriateness (e.g., Birney, Beckmann, & Seah, in press). Although a creative output can be evaluated on such a unidimensional continuum, this does not indicate that it results from a single ability (Barbot & Tinio, 2015). Componential approaches have posited that creativity results from people's unique combination of multiple resources coming into play in creative work, including aspects of cognition, motivation, and personality (e.g., Lubart, 1999; Sternberg & Lubart, 1995).

NEW DIRECTIONS FOR CHILD AND ADOLESCENT DEVELOPMENT • DOI: 10.1002/cad

Extending this view and extant "hybrid" models of creativity (e.g., Kaufman & Baer, 2004; Plucker & Beghetto, 2004), we have recently posited that this set of person-level resources interacts with each particular creative task's characteristics and demands and that, ultimately, a person's creative potential will depend on the "quality of fit" between her unique profile of resources and the demands of a given creative task (e.g., Barbot & Tinio, 2015; Barbot et al., 2015; Lubart, Zenasni, & Barbot, 2013). By extension, this view suggests that a person has as many potentials for creativity as there are creative tasks (i.e., outlets in which outcomes can be evaluated on the creativity continuum). With the same unique profile of resources, a person can show high potential for poetry writing, average potential for fiction writing, and low potential for musical composition. This heterogeneity is expected because these creative outlets rely conceptually on a different mixture of person-level resources. Because a given creative task may rely on a very specific combination of resources, the likelihood that a person's profile of resources optimally fits that task's requirement is very low. As a result, the probability of achieving an outstanding level of creativity in that task is very low and most outcomes will be of average or low creativity (depending on how "misfitting" the person's profile of resources is to the task's requirements). Furthermore, it is likely that a person's creative potential will never lead to creative achievement in a given task (regardless of the quality of fit between her potential and that task) if she doesn't have the opportunity to engage in that task or doesn't choose to invest time and energy in that task (e.g., Amabile, 1996).

This *"optimal-fit view"* helps understand the rarity of exceptional creativity outcomes (big-C creativity) while shedding light on the issue of domain generality-specificity of creativity (i.e., it is not likely that multiple creative tasks across domains will require the same "optimal" combination of resources). It should, however, not be strictly interpreted as if each person's profile of resources is static or could be compared to a "winning bingo ticket" when interacting with the right task (i.e., suggesting that everybody could show outstanding creativity, provided that they are completing their "best fitting task"[1]). Importantly, individual inclinations, interests, and personal investments remain at the center of creative work and are deeply and continuously shaped by environmental influences and experiences. These influences (which can be seen as part of the person's potential for creativity) may at least partly explain patterns of discontinuity of creativity throughout the life span.

Discontinuity of the Development of Creative Potential

Because creativity is multifaceted and partly domain- (and task-) specific, creative potential does not develop as a monolithic entity: it is multidimensional and each task-specific potential results from the development of multiple contributing person-level resources. Among them, divergent thinking

(DT) is by far the most widely studied from a developmental perspective. DT is the ability to produce multiple solutions or ideas in response to a single problem or stimulus, such as generating alternative uses for a common object. Recent research has focused on DT of preschool children as young as two years old (Bijvoet-van den Berg & Hoicka, 2014) and concluded that individual differences in DT start emerging during preschool age, and then, DT performance tends to increase. This general trend seems to continue until about age 40, followed by "systematic maturational declines" (McCrae, Arenberg, & Costa, 1987; p. 136), and is punctuated by multiple patterns of discontinuity, especially during childhood and adolescence.

Based on several longitudinal and cross-cultural studies, Torrance (1967) produced a comprehensive report on the issue of DT development and discontinuity from childhood to early adolescence. The general trend described by Torrance, confirmed by several subsequent studies, can be summarized by an overall increase of DT from preschool age to early adolescence with three common "slumps" (steep and temporary decrease in DT performance). The first slump occurs around age five, the second around age nine (fourth-grade slump), and the third around age 12. These slumps, and in particular the fourth-grade slump, have received substantial attention despite issues of replicability, cross-cultural differences, and considerable individual differences regarding the existence, timing, and domain in which a slump is or is not observed.

As an illustration, Charles and Runco (2001) identified a significant peak, rather than slump, in the divergent thinking of fourth-grade children. Lau and Cheung (2010) did not identify a fourth-grade slump of Chinese students, but rather, sixth- and seventh-grade slumps, with marked gender differences in developmental patterns of DT. Similarly, Besançon and Lubart (2008) demonstrated a different timing of the slumps of French children in middle school that seemed to vary according to the pedagogical context and the nature of the task administered. Claxton, Pannells, and Rhoads (2005) identified a decrease of the cognitive aspects of creativity at the onset of puberty, similar to Yi, Hu, Plucker, and McWilliams (2013) which showed a general decline of DT for Chinese students between ages 12 and 14, followed by an increase of small magnitude. In contrast, Kleibeuker, De Dreu, and Crone (2013) showed a relative peak of visuospatial DT around 15 years old, but no age-related difference in verbal DT.

Other person-level resources that contribute to creative potential have been investigated and, similar to developmental patterns of DT, have often been described by nonlinear trajectories. In adolescence, insight ability seems to increase with age (Kleibeuker et al., 2013), as does the accuracy of original idea selection and the preference for appropriate ideas (Charles & Runco, 2001). Claxton and colleagues (2005) have suggested a peak of divergent-related variables (including curiosity, complexity, or risk taking) around ninth grade that appears in the same wave as a slump in DT. These patterns are consistent with research showing how motivational dimensions and personality trait development contribute to variability in the developmental trajectory of creative potential in various domains (Hong, Peng, & O'Neil, 2014). Personality development could, in addition, follow different developmental pathways according to gender, reflecting differences in the timing of the psychosocial stages experienced by girls and boys. For example, openness to experience related to creative potential in music, visual arts, and creative writing (but less to science and technology; Hong et al., 2014) shows an increasing trend in adolescent girls and a decreasing one in adolescent boys (e.g., Branje, van Lieshout, & Gerris, 2007). Internalized age-related stereotypes (and perhaps gender-related stereotypes), and age-related differentiation in beliefs about personality development could also affect the expression of personality features related to creativity (Hui et al., 2014). Hence, it is expected that boys and girls differ in their creative potential development in various creative outlets based upon multiple conative variables that follow distinct developmental trajectories.

As a last example, domain-specific expertise and domain-based knowledge, crucial for creative achievement, can also be described by nonmonotonic longitudinal trends. Based on a historiometric analysis of 59 classical composers, Simonton (2000) suggests that complex specialization and versatility effects determine creative development across the life span of eminent creative persons. This "creative-expertise" hypothesis could easily apply to everyday life creativity, as found in children and adolescents, given the necessary contribution of domain-based knowledge in any creative work.

Foundations of Individual Differences in Creativity Development

As outlined previously, there is discontinuity in the development of creativity during childhood and adolescence with "slumps" frequently cited. However, there is variability as to whether or not a given child will experience the slump, when it is experienced, in which type of creative outlet the slump is experienced, and the outcome of the slump (some children might not "recover" after experiencing a slump; Charles & Runco, 2001; Runco, 2014). These differences can be explained by three sets of complementary explanations: (a) asynchronicity (asynchronous development of individual resources involved in creative potential), (b) environmental influences, and (c) task specificity (creative task characteristics and other methodological artifacts).

Asynchronicity. Patterns of discontinuity can be understood in light of the "natural," and partly genetically grounded, development of the various resources that contribute to creative potential (Barbot, Tan, & Grigorenko, 2013). Using a "stage" approach, Piaget suggested that children through fourth grade are developmentally "concrete thinkers," which aligns with the idea of the fourth-grade slump, as children remain consistent with reality and fail to propose ideas that are more original. Approaches that have relied on "waves of development" have suggested that not all components of the mind are developing at the same time and that the weakening of creative thinking could be related to the emergence of new skills in other areas. In this line, Lubart and Lautrey (1996) showed a fourth-grade slump in DT associated with a substantial increase in logical reasoning. They interpreted this result as a compensating effect, in which the "wave" of DT might be in a "slump" when the wave of reasoning is at its "peak" (see also Guignard & Lubart, in press). Many similar examples can be found in the neurodevelopmental literature, highlighting, for example, a temporal gap between the development of the socioemotional system and the cognitive control systems in adolescence, leading to maladaptive behavior such as risk taking and impulsivity (e.g., Barbot & Hunter, 2012), which could also have implications for the development of person-level resources important for creativity.

Environmental Influences. According to Torrance (1968) creativity slumps can be explained by normative effects of the school environment, as they happen at times when children are taught to respect school rules and fit within the classroom norms. This explanation finds support in research showing slumps at different points in time depending on the specific contextual and cultural demands. For example, Yi and colleagues (2013) suggest that the emphasis on college entrance exams taken during high school in China raises expectations for academic performance in middle school, explaining cultural differences in DT trajectories (pressures have moved into earlier grades in this culture). These effects can be moderated by teachers' influences (Davies et al., 2014) and the type of pedagogy encouraged (Besançon & Lubart, 2008; Besançon, Lubart, & Barbot, 2013).

The family environment is also a critical determinant of creative potential development. Here, too, the cultural context has an indirect influence through common parental practices that are prevalent in a culture (Mourgues, Barbot, Tan, & Grigorenko, 2014). For example, Fearon, Copeland, and Saxon (2013) noted the negative impact of authoritarian parenting, a common parenting style in Jamaican culture, on the development of creativity in Jamaican youth. Consistent with prior research on parenting and creativity, this result is in line with the idea that creativity flourishes when developmental experiences and conditions are optimal (Dai et al., 2012; Runco & Cayirdag, 2013).

Recent research, however, tends to challenge this assumption. For example, Dahlman, Bäckström, Bohlin, and Frans (2013) show that street children in Bolivia were far more efficient in specific DT tasks (generating alternative uses of a common object) compared to children of low socioeconomic status (SES) living with their parents. They concluded that street children gained "training" in this type of tasks given the nature of their daily-life experience (perhaps requiring some of the skills engaged by alternative uses tasks). Similarly, Damian and Simonton (2015) make the hypothesis that experiences of developmental adversity (such as early parental death, poverty, or psychopathology) might foster unconventional ideas. Based on an analysis of eminent African Americans, they concluded that "diversifying experiences" push people outside the realm of "normality" and in turn influence the development of creativity.

Together, this body of work supports the joint contribution of individual and environmental influences to creativity development (Niu, 2007). Because the influence of the school and family environment is not systematic and because the status of adversity as a condition that impedes creativity development is unclear, environment-level resources should be further explored and considered in their interaction with person-level resources (e.g., "absorption level" of environmental influences), as well as with task requirements.

Task Specificity and Methodological Artifacts. Several methodological limitations and artifacts contribute to the apparent discontinuity of the development of creativity. First, developmental studies of creativity suffer often from small sample sizes, selection biases (alternative tracks underrepresented), and the use of cross-sectional designs (focusing on age-group differences), making it difficult to untangle cohort effects from actual developmental effects. Even longitudinally, classroom and teachers' effects outlined earlier could bias developmental inferences (it is not likely that participants will "benefit" equally from these effects from grade to grade).

Most important, the different nature and emphasis of tasks used in studies may explain variations in the existence and timing of slumps (Charles & Runco, 2001): almost all studies that have administered multiple tasks to the same participants have outlined distinct developmental trajectories for each task (Besançon & Lubart, 2008; Claxton et al., 2005; Kleibeuker et al., 2013; Torrance, 1968), confirming that not all tasks are equivalent when it comes to measuring creative potential (specific demands vary as a function of the task, even within the same domain of production; Wu, Cheng, Ip, & McBride-Chang, 2005).

In a related way, one of the most challenging issues in longitudinal studies of creativity is the reliance on similar but nonparallel tasks at different measurement occasions. Because production-based tasks require producing original and unique outputs, administering strictly the same task at multiple measurement occasions makes little sense: "memory" effects, carry-over effects, and other "learning" biases may lead to rote production of outputs already proposed by the child or traded with a classmate at an earlier testing session. However, by exposing children to a slightly different task at each measurement occasion (e.g., alternative uses for a brick vs. a cardboard box), it becomes challenging to isolate a person's "true change" in the tested ability as distinct from change related to variations in the task's characteristics. Indeed, these characteristics may not have a systematic effect: at a given time, one may be more "inspired" when providing alternative uses for a brick rather than for a cardboard box. This is highlighted by the large proportion of task-specific variance in creative potential tests scores, as suggested by low to moderate inter-task correlations (Barbot, Besançon, & Lubart, in press; Dumas & Dunbar, 2014).

Toward an Optimal-Fit View of Creative Potential in Development

As outlined by Simonton (2000), "at any given time, the performance outcome for a particular work in a specified form or genre will be contingent on a chaotic mixture of influences, some beneficial and others deleterious" (p. 313). This mechanism is likely to occur at every level of the creativity continuum, including in "everyday" accomplishments of children and adolescents. Specifically, we have posited earlier that individual differences in creativity outcomes result from the interaction between individual-level resources and task-specific demands. This *"optimal-fit"* view translates easily in a developmental perspective: performance outcomes in a given creative outlet will depend upon the specific creative-task characteristics and the (asynchronous) development of person-level characteristics (e.g., DT and other cognitive factors, personality, motivational and emotional characteristics). At different points in time, the resulting multivariate profile of person-level resources will be more or less in line with the particular task requirements, leading to outcomes of variable creativity over time. This idea is illustrated in Figure 3.1.

As shown in Figure 3.1a, the various person-level resources of a child develop asynchronously from childhood to adolescence following distinct trajectories (for the sake of clarity, only the hypothetical development of selected resources is represented). Figure 3.1b represents two tasks' characteristics in terms of required level of these person-level resources. Finally, Figure 3.1c illustrates the "quality of fit" between the child's multivariate profile of person-level resources at different point in time and requirements of tasks A and B. This quality of fit represents the child's creative potential for each "target" task (Figure 3.1b). As shown, the hypothetical child may have a higher creative potential for task B than for task A at 10 years age: the quality of fit between the child's profile of resources and task B's demands is better than for task A's demands. However, at 12 years age, the quality of fit has diminished due to the "natural" development of the child's profile of resources. This profile is now more aligned with task A's demands than with task B's.

Environmental influences are not incorporated in this illustration but they could be represented as forces that steer each person-level resource in various directions, depending on their interaction with these resources. Hence, environmental influences have an indirect effect on creative potential in a given task (Figure 3.1c) through their beneficial (or harmful) influence on each person-level resource.

NEW DIRECTIONS FOR CHILD AND ADOLESCENT DEVELOPMENT • DOI: 10.1002/cad

Figure 3.1. Illustration of the "Optimal-Fit" View of Creativity Development

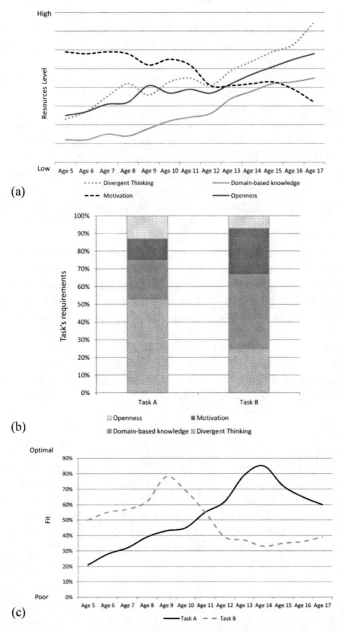

(a)

(b)

(c)

Note: (a) Development of four person-level resources during childhood and adolescence. (b) Two tasks' characteristics in terms of person-level requirements. (c) "Quality of fit" between the individual's multivariate profile of person-level resources (3.1a) and tasks' characteristics (3.1b).

Conclusion

In this article, we have outlined an *"optimal-fit"* view of creativity according to which the creativity of a product depends on the fit between a creative task characteristic and a person's profile of resources underlying creativity in that task. By extension, the apparent discontinuity of the development of creativity in childhood and adolescence can be understood in light of (a) asynchronous development of person-level resources contributing to creativity, (b) environmental influences (orienting the development of person-level resources), and (c) task characteristics.

We have also outlined a number of conceptual and methodological limitations to studies on the development of creativity, and, in particular, the need to capture its multidimensional and partly domain-specific nature as it develops: the development of creativity is not a generalized process, as creativity is not equivalent to the sum of its constituting "ingredients" and certainly not equivalent to a single ingredient, such as DT. Additionally, we have pointed out the critical need for longitudinal evidence rather than age-group comparisons.

These endeavors may prove particularly challenging given common issues of task-specificity and repeated measurements or untangling cohorts and classroom effects from true change. Therefore, it follows that important directions for the field are (a) the development of new measures specially designed for longitudinal studies (e.g., limiting the contribution of task-specific factors), or devising new scoring methods for existing instrument that would reduce common biases when used longitudinally, and (b) the development of methodological and statistical paradigms that would control for high task-specificity and other methodological biases impeding the study of "true change" in creativity research.

Author Notes

The preparation of this article was supported by grant RFP-15-05 to Baptiste Barbot and Franck Zenasni from the Imagination Institute (www.imagination-institute.org), funded by the John Templeton Foundation. The opinions expressed in this publication are those of the authors and do not necessarily reflect the view of the Imagination Institute or the John Templeton Foundation. We thank Kristen Piering and Brianna Heuser for editorial assistance in the preparation of this manuscript.

Note

1. This view would be inaccurate because some people might have consistently low creative outcomes across tasks as their profile of resources may consistently misfit any creative task requirements. This approach is empirically testable by (a) identifying the optimal level of resources associated with high creativity outcomes in a given task, which can be determined by modeling the average profile of resources of people who demonstrated high achievement in that task (e.g., Caroff & Lubart, 2012) or by expert

elicitation techniques (e.g., Barbot, Tan, Randi, Santa-Donato, & Grigorenko, 2012), and then (b) evaluating the distance between the person's multivariate profile of resources and the determined "optimal" profile of resources (Lubart et al., 2013).

References

Amabile, T. M. (1996). *Creativity in context*. Boulder, CO: Westview.

Baer, J. (1998). The case for domain specificity in creativity. *Creativity Research Journal*, *11*, 173–177.

Barbot, B., Besançon, M., & Lubart, T. (2015). Creative potential in educational settings: Its nature, measure, and nurture. *Education 3–13*, *43*(4), 371–381. doi:10.1080/03004279.2015.1020643

Barbot, B., Besançon, M., & Lubart, T. (in press). *The generality-specificity of creativity: Exploring the structure of creative potential with EPoC*. Learning and Individual Differences.

Barbot, B., & Hunter, S. R. (2012). Developmental changes in adolescence and risks for delinquency. In E. L. Grigorenko (Ed.), *Handbook of juvenile forensic psychology and psychiatry* (pp. 11–34). New York: Springer. doi:10.1007/978-1-4614-0905-2

Barbot, B., Tan, M., & Grigorenko, E. L. (2013). The genetics of creativity: The generative and receptive sides of the creativity equation. In O. Vartanian, A. Bristol, & J. C. Kaufman (Eds.), *The neuroscience of creativity* (pp. 71–93). Cambridge, MA: MIT Press.

Barbot, B., Tan, M., Randi, J., Santa-Donato, G., & Grigorenko, E. L. (2012). Essential skills for creative writing: Integrating multiple domain-specific perspectives. *Thinking Skills and Creativity*, *7*(3), 209–223. doi:10.1016/j.tsc.2012.04.006

Barbot, B., & Tinio, P. P. L. (2015). Where is the "g" in creativity? A specialization-differentiation hypothesis. *Frontiers in Human Neuroscience*, *8*(1041). doi:10.3389/fnhum.2014.01041

Besançon, M., & Lubart, T. I. (2008). Differences in the development of creative competencies in children schooled in diverse learning environments. *Learning and Individual Differences*, *18*(4), 381–389.

Besançon, M., Lubart, T. I., & Barbot, B. (2013). Creative giftedness and educational opportunities. *Educational and Child Psychology*, *30*(2), 79–88.

Bijvoet-van den Berg, S., & Hoicka, E. (2014). Individual differences and age-related changes in divergent thinking in toddlers and preschoolers. *Developmental Psychology*, *50*(6), 1629–1639. doi:10.1037/a0036131

Birney, D. P., Beckmann, J. F., & Seah, Y. Z. (in press). More than the eye of the beholder: The interplay of person, task and situation factors in evaluative judgments of creativity. *Learning and Individual Differences*. doi:10.1016/j.lindif.2015.07.007

Branje, S. J. T., van Lieshout, C. F. M., & Gerris, J. R. M. (2007). Big five personality development in adolescence and adulthood. *European Journal of Personality*, *21*(1), 45–62.

Caroff, X., & Lubart, T. I. (2012). Multidimensional approach to detecting creative potential in managers. *Creativity Research Journal*, *24*(1), 13–20. doi:10.1080/10400419.2012.652927

Charles, R. E., & Runco, M. A. (2001). Developmental trends in the evaluative and divergent thinking of children. *Creativity Research Journal*, *13*(3), 417–437.

Claxton, A. F., Pannells, T. C., & Rhoads, P. A. (2005). Developmental trends in the creativity of school-age children. *Creativity Research Journal*, *17*(4), 327–335. doi:10.1207/s15326934crj1704_4

Dahlman, S., Bäckström, P., Bohlin, G., & Frans, Ö. (2013). Cognitive abilities of street children: Low-SES Bolivian boys with and without experience of living in the street. *Child Neuropsychology*, *19*(5), 540–556.

Dai, D. Y., Tan, X., Marathe, D., Valtcheva, A., Pruzek, R. M., & Shen, J. (2012). Influences of social and educational environments on creativity during adolescence: Does SES matter? *Creativity Research Journal, 24*(2–3), 191–199.

Damian, R. I., & Simonton, D. K. (2015). Psychopathology, adversity, and creativity: Diversifying experiences in the development of eminent African-Americans. *Journal of Personality and Social Psychology, 108*(4), 623–636. doi:10.1037/pspi0000011

Davies, D., Jindal-Snape, D., Digby, R., Howe, A., Collier, C., & Hay, P. (2014). The roles and development needs of teachers to promote creativity: A systematic review of literature. *Teaching and Teacher Education, 41*, 34–41. doi:10.1016/j.tate.2014.03.003

Dumas, D., & Dunbar, K. N. (2014). Understanding fluency and originality: A latent variable perspective. *Thinking Skills and Creativity, 14*, 56–67. doi:10.1016/j.tsc.2014.09.003

Fearon, D. D., Copeland, D., & Saxon, T. F. (2013). The relationship between parenting styles and creativity in a sample of Jamaican children. *Creativity Research Journal, 25*(1), 119–128.

Guignard, J., & Lubart, T. (in press). Creativity and reason: Friends or foes? In J. C. Kaufman & J. Baer (Eds.), *Creativity and reason in cognitive development. The Cambridge companion to creativity and reason in cognitive development* (2nd ed.). New York: Cambridge University Press.

Hong, E., Peng, Y., & O'Neil H. F. Jr., (2014). Activities and accomplishments in various domains: Relationships with creative personality and creative motivation in adolescence. *Roeper Review, 36*(2), 92–103. doi:10.1080/02783193.2014.884199

Hui, A. N., Yeung, D. Y., Sue-Chan, C., Chan, K., Hui, D. C., & Cheng, S. (2014). Gains and losses in creative personality as perceived by adults across the life span. *Translational Issues in Psychological Science, 1*(S), 28–34. doi:10.1037/2332-2136.1.S.28

Kaufman, J. C., & Baer, J. (2004). The Amusement Park Theoretical (APT) Model of creativity. *Korean Journal of Thinking and Problem Solving, 14*, 15–25.

Kleibeuker, S. W., De Dreu, C. K., & Crone, E. A. (2013). The development of creative cognition across adolescence: Distinct trajectories for insight and divergent thinking. *Developmental Science, 16*(1), 2–12.

Lau, S., & Cheung, P. C. (2010). Developmental trends of creativity: What twists of turn do boys and girls take at different grades? *Creativity Research Journal, 22*(3), 329–336.

Lubart, T. I. (1999). Componential models of creativity. In M. A. Runco, & S. Pritzker (Eds.), *Encyclopedia of creativity* (Vol. 1, pp. 295–300). New York: Academic Press.

Lubart, T. I., & Lautrey, J. (1996). Development of creativity in 9- to 10-year old children. Paper presented at the Growing Mind Congress, Geneva, Switzerland.

Lubart, T. I., Zenasni, F., & Barbot, B. (2013). Creative potential and its measurement. *International Journal of Talent Development and Creativity, 1*(2), 41–51.

McCrae, R. R., Arenberg, D., & Costa, P. T. (1987). Declines in divergent thinking with age: Cross-sectional, longitudinal, and cross-sequential analyses. *Psychology and Aging, 2*(2), 130–137. doi:10.1037/0882-7974.2.2.130

Mourgues, C., Barbot, B., Tan, M., & Grigorenko, E. L. (2014). The interaction between culture and the development of creativity. In L. A. Jensen (Ed.), *The Oxford handbook of human development and culture: An interdisciplinary perspective* (pp. 255–270). New York: Oxford University Press. doi:10.1093/oxfordhb/9780199948550.013.16

Niu, W. (2007). Individual and environmental influences on Chinese student creativity. *The Journal of Creative Behavior, 41*(3), 151–175. doi:10.1002/j.2162-6057.2007.tb01286.x

Plucker, J. A., & Beghetto, R. A. (2004). Why creativity is domain general, why it looks domain specific, and why the distinction doesn't matter. In R. J. Sternberg, E. L. Grigorenko, & J. L. Singer (Eds.), *Creativity: From potential to realization* (pp. 153–168). Washington, DC: American Psychological Association.

Runco, M. A. (2014). *Creativity. Theories and themes: Research, development, and practice* (2nd ed.). Waltham, MA: Elsevier.

Runco, M. A., & Cayirdag, N. (2013). The development of children's creativity. In O. N. Saracho & B. Spodek (Eds.), *Handbook of research on the education of young children* (3rd ed., pp. 102–114). New York: Routledge.

Simonton, D. K. (2000). Creative development as acquired expertise: Theoretical issues and an empirical test. *Developmental Review, 20*(2), 283–318.

Sternberg, R. J., & Lubart, T. I. (1995). *Defying the crowd: Cultivating creativity in a culture of conformity.* New York: Free Press.

Torrance, E. P. (1967). *Understanding the fourth grade slump in creative thinking* (Report No. BR-5-0508; CRP-994). Washington, DC: U.S. Office of Education.

Torrance, E. P. (1968). A longitudinal examination of the fourth grade slump in creativity. *Gifted Child Quarterly, 12*(4), 195–199.

Wallach, M. A. (1970). Creativity. In P. H. Mussen (Ed.), *Carmichael's manual of child psychology* (Vol. 1, pp. 1211–1272). New York: Wiley.

Wu, C. H., Cheng, Y., Ip, H. M., & McBride-Chang, C. (2005). Age differences in creativity: Task structure and knowledge base. *Creativity Research Journal, 17*(4), 321–326. doi:10.1207/s15326934crj1704_3

Yi, X., Hu, W., Plucker, J. A., & McWilliams, J. (2013). Is there a developmental slump in creativity in China? The relationship between organizational climate and creativity development in Chinese adolescents. *Journal of Creative Behavior, 47*(1), 22–40.

BAPTISTE BARBOT *is an assistant professor in psychology at the Department of Psychology, Pace University, New York, NY, and an adjunct assistant professor at the Child Study Center, Yale University, New Haven, CT.*

TODD I. LUBART *is professor of psychology at the Université Paris Descartes, and director of the LATI, Paris, France.*

MAUD BESANÇON *is an assistant professor in psychology at the Université Paris Ouest, Nanterre, France.*

NEW DIRECTIONS FOR CHILD AND ADOLESCENT DEVELOPMENT • DOI: 10.1002/cad

Kornilov, S. A., Kornilova, T. V., & Grigorenko, E. L. (2016). The cross-cultural invariance of creative cognition: A case study of creative writing in U.S. and Russian college students. In B. Barbot (Ed.), *Perspectives on creativity development. New Directions for Child and Adolescent Development, 151,* 47–59.

4

The Cross-Cultural Invariance of Creative Cognition: A Case Study of Creative Writing in U.S. and Russian College Students

Sergey A. Kornilov, Tatiana V. Kornilova, Elena L. Grigorenko

Abstract

Unlike intelligence, creativity has rarely been investigated from the standpoint of cross-cultural invariance of the structure of the instruments used to measure it. In the study reported in this article, we investigated the cross-cultural invariance of expert ratings of creative stories written by undergraduate students from the Russian Federation and the United States. Analyses of differential rater and item functioning using Many-Facet Rasch Measurement and multiple levels of invariance using confirmatory factor analyses suggested partial measurement invariance of creative ability estimates obtained using this method in two cultures. Russian and U.S. students demonstrated similar overall levels of creativity; however, U.S. students received higher emotionality ratings than Russian students did. The findings are discussed in the context of viewing creativity as at least a partially culturally invariant trait whose manifestation is moderated by culture-specific semantic knowledge and patterns of linguistic behavior. © 2016 Wiley Periodicals, Inc.

NEW DIRECTIONS FOR CHILD AND ADOLESCENT DEVELOPMENT, no. 151, Spring 2016 © 2016 Wiley Periodicals, Inc.
Published online in Wiley Online Library (wileyonlinelibrary.com). • DOI: 10.1002/cad.20149

C reativity is widely recognized as an inherently cultural phenomenon, embedded in a complex network of environmental influences. Thus, definitions of creativity often explicitly or implicitly mention culture as the key contextual element that both (a) shapes creativity as an ability that depends on the functioning of convergent and divergent processes and the acquisition of knowledge, and (b) serves as the necessary framework for the evaluation of the products resulting from the application of this ability in a specific task context. Underscoring the role of culture in the development and manifestation of creativity mandates the investigation of the complex interactions between cognitive processes that support creativity and symbolic, behavioral, ideational, and value patterns transmitted and internalized through exposure to a particular culture (Kroeber & Kluckhon, 1952) and its specific contexts, including family and school (Mourgues, Barbot, Tan, & Grigorenko, 2014). These interactions are hypothesized to result in the development of the ability to create novel, original, elaborated, and task as well as culturally appropriate ideas, solutions, and products. Crucially, the requirement for the creative product to be culturally appropriate (and effective; see Runco & Jaeger, 2012, for a discussion on the standard definition of creativity) reflects the existence of substantial differences in the previously mentioned symbolic and value patterns across different cultures, and has important implications for our understanding of the nature of this ability as well as our approaches to measuring it.

Studies of cross-cultural differences in creativity mainly revolve around the examination of conceptions of creativity across different cultures, cross-cultural variation in personality traits that are viewed as characteristic of a "creative person," and direct evaluation of creative ability across diverse cultures that generally hinges on the evaluation of the characteristics of a particular creative product. With respect to conceptions of creativity, the general consensus is that there are properties or features of creativity that are recognized as key across multiple cultures—most notably specific cognitive processes (e.g., divergent thinking) and personality traits (e.g., risk taking and perseverance) that contribute to creativity (Erez & Nouri, 2010), and characteristics of the "final" creative product such as novelty/originality and its adaptive value/task appropriateness (Lubart, 2010). However, cultures have been found to differ with respect to the relative emphasis that they place on specific characteristics of the product (i.e., novelty vs. adaptation) and/or on the ways they regulate the specifics of the implementation of these characteristics (Rubera, Ordanini, & Griffith, 2011; Sternberg & Lubart, 1995).

Both the relative emphasis on different features of creativity across cultures and the cultural specificity of the actual manifestation of these features reflect the impact of the cultural expectations regarding what is considered creative and why. Although multiple accounts of how these expectations shape creativity have been developed, they mostly concern the so-called *Big C* or eminent creativity—the types of creative cognition and products that reshape the culture from within. However, much less is known with respect to the extent that these cultural influences are manifested in the *little c* (i.e., in individual differences in creative ability estimates viewed through the lens of the rater evaluation of task-specific creative products).

The study reported in this article attempts to address this gap in the literature by examining the cross-cultural differences in the ratings of creative products produced by Russian and U.S. college students. However, instead of focusing on the group differences in creative ability estimates obtained by the two groups of students, we focused our attention on the internal structure and psychometric properties of the writing task we used to elicit creative stories. Correspondingly, we examined the cross-cultural invariance of creative cognition in the domain of creative writing. Such an examination serves the purpose of illuminating the extent to which the cognitive architecture of verbal creativity is similar across the two cultures (in the context when the same process is realized through the means of distinct symbolic and linguistic systems the use of which is culturally regulated), and whether there are dimensions of creative cognition (measured through product) that are particularly amenable to cultural influences. We performed this investigation within the psychometric paradigm, focusing our attention on (a) construct invariance—the extent to which creative ability, as measured by the Creative Stories task—exhibits similar internal structure in the two samples of students and (b) differential item functioning (DIF), traditionally viewed as indicating the presence of a local and specific bias in particular elements of creative ability that cannot be attributed to overall group differences in creative ability.

Methods

Our quasi-experimental study focused on the cross-cultural invariance of verbal creativity ratings obtained through administering an open-ended creativity task (see below) in two samples of undergraduates attending colleges in Russian Federation and the United States.

Participants. One thousand undergraduate students participated in the study—500 from Moscow State University (MSU; in the age range from 18 to 60 years, with $M = 21.11$, $SD = 4.78$; 390 were females), Russian Federation, and 500 from the University of California in San Bernardino (UCSB) and San Francisco (UCSF), United States, in the age range from 17 to 58 years ($M = 24.97$, $SD = 6.29$; 325 females). Of these, after the removal of missing data, responses were provided by 318 Russian and 346 U.S. students, for the total effective sample of 664.

The analyses capitalized on two existing datasets: the U.S. sample constituted part of the Transitions in the Development of Giftedness project (Sternberg et al., 2007) data, whereas the Russian sample was recruited for the cross-cultural investigation of the psychometric properties of some of the assessments used by Sternberg et al. (2007; the complete description of the sample can be found in Kornilov & Grigorenko, 2010).

Creative Stories Task. All participants were administered an open-ended creative writing task called Creative Stories. According to the task procedure, participants were asked to write a brief creative story in 15 minutes using one of the five offered titles: "Two Chatting Spiders," "The Fishing Moose," "A Spotted Creature," "A Banana with Many Peels," and "The Reading Dragon." Participants were instructed to use only one of the titles in their story and to write as creatively as possible to maximize performance.

The written stories were rated for creativity according to four key dimensions (hereafter, items) using the comprehensive scoring rubrics manual developed by the Transitions in the Development of Giftedness project team (Sternberg et al., 2007) based on Sternberg's investment theory of creativity (Sternberg, 2012). Thus, the stories were rated on *Originality* (novelty, uniqueness, and unexpectedness of the story plot and its elements, individualized for each title), *Complexity* (of story structure, form/writing, and imagery), *Emotionality* (incorporation of emotion in the story and elicitation of emotions from the reader), and *Task Appropriateness* (whether the story is sufficiently descriptive and related to the title in a clear and logical manner). Each story was rated on the four dimensions using a five-category polytomous rating scale. Each category was supplemented by a detailed description of the scoring criteria (e.g., to receive a score of 4 on Complexity, the story had to have a solid and elaborated structure with imagery that the rater could describe as "striking" in at least one instance) and examples.

The stories generated by U.S. students were scored by two raters using a rating plan with an overlap of k = 30 written stories. The stories generated by Russian students were scored by three raters with the overlap of k = 100 stories. A set of k = 60 stories from the U.S. sample was also scored by one bilingual rater who scored stories from the Russian sample. All raters underwent extensive training prior to scoring the stories to reach acceptable within-country agreement levels (Pearson's r = .60 or Cohen's K = .50 for each element). Within- and between-country interrater reliabilities are presented in the Results section (Table 4.1).

Table 4.1. Interrater Reliabilities for the Creative Stories Task Scores

Item	Russian Raters		U.S. Raters		Russian and U.S. Raters	
	r	Cohen's K	r	Cohen's K	r	Cohen's K
Originality	.95	.92	.63	.50	.64	.21
Complexity	.90	.86	.94	.85	.54	.34
Emotionality	.75	.71	.97	.89	.54	.10
Descriptiveness	.95	.90	.87	.63	.65	.29

Note: Estimates represent averages of pairwise estimates obtained for each pair of raters who rated the same story; r = Pearson's correlation coefficient; Cohen's K = Cohen's Kappa (chance-adjusted agreement coefficient).

The raters were instructed to be lenient and assign the higher score when in doubt.

Analytical Approach. The analysis was performed in two distinct yet related frameworks. First, we analyzed the data using a Many-Facet Rasch Measurement (MFRM) model as implemented in Facets for Windows (Linacre, 2009). Briefly, this approach uses a unified conjoint measurement item response theory (IRT) model to obtain stable calibrations of multiple facets on a common scale, e.g., estimates of student ability (creativity), rater severity, and item difficulty. We analyzed the data using a five-facet MFRM rating scale model with students, items, raters, titles, and country designated as separate facets.

Crucially, MFRM enables the investigation of systematic biases in expert ratings by performing differential facet analysis (DFF; Bond & Fox, 2007). We used DFF analysis to establish the invariance of item difficulty (differential item functioning, DIF) and rater severity (differential rater functioning, DRF) parameters in the U.S. and the Russian samples within the same model, and we used the omnibus test for the presence of DFF elements as well as the t criterion to test each interaction parameter separately. First, the measures for all facets and the structure of the rating scale were calibrated and fixed; at the second step, the expected values for observations were subtracted from observed values, and residuals corresponding to each interaction term were integrated and transformed into DFF bias estimates. The DFF parameters were tested for statistical significance using the t statistic (using the standard Bonferroni procedure to correct for multiple statistical testing at $\alpha = .05$), and their overall impact was evaluated with the omnibus test for the presence of DFF items (Linacre, 2009) and percentage of variance in creativity ratings attributable to DFF.

We also analyzed the cross-cultural invariance of the Creative Stories task through multigroup maximum-likelihood confirmatory factor analysis (CFA) as implemented in EQS for Windows (Bentler, 1995) using the robust maximum likelihood estimation. Briefly, cross-cultural invariance testing within the CFA framework proceeds via the iterative comparison of nested CFA models with progressively stringent sets of constraints (Byrne, 2006) at each of the following levels of invariance: configural (equivalence of the number of latent factors and patterns of factor loadings in two groups), metric (magnitude of factor loadings in two groups), scalar (equivalence of indicators intercepts), and residual (equivalence of error variances). When more than one rater's scores were available for a particular participant, the scores were averaged prior to the analysis.

Results

As mentioned above, the analyses reported in this section focused on the interrater reliability of scores obtained for the Creative Stories task, its cross-cultural invariance, and the presence of differential item functioning.

Interrater Reliability. The interrater reliabilities are presented in Table 4.1. Overall, the raters demonstrated high interrater agreement levels within groups (mean $r = .89$ and $.85$ for Russian and U.S. raters, respectively). Although the interrater reliabilities between the Russian and the U.S. raters were lower (r ranged from $.54$ to $.64$ for the four key dimensions), it was still at an acceptable level. Analyses of Cohen's K (Cohen, 1960) suggested that within-country chance-corrected reliabilities were in the moderate to substantial (Landis & Koch, 1977) range (from $.71$ to $.92$ for Russian raters; from $.50$ to $.89$ for U.S. raters); however, agreement was lower between the Russian and the U.S. raters (with the lowest estimate for Emotionality, $.10$).

Many-Facet Rasch Modeling. To further investigate whether there were systematic biases in the scores of the rater who scored the stories from both countries, we fitted a unidimensional five-facet MFRM model to the data.

The model explained 60.2% of variance in the Creative Stories scores obtained by the students. The person reliability index (estimated reproducibility of relative measure location, interpreted similarly to Cronbach's alpha; Linacre, 1997) was high at $.85$, and the model reliably differentiated between at least three levels of performance (separation index $= 2.42$). The analysis of local fit indices did not reveal items, raters, or story titles that violated model assumptions (all InfitMS < 1.37, all OutfitMS < 1.34; values between 0.50 and 1.50 generally suggest acceptable measurement quality; Wright & Masters, 1990; see Table 4.2) indicating overall satisfactory measurement properties of the task as applied to our samples.

Table 4.2. Resulting Facet Element Parameters for the MFRM Model of Creative Stories

		Average	Est.	SE	Infit	Outfit
Country	US	2.93	.51	.04	.99	1.03
	RUS	2.65	.51	.02	1.02	1.01
Item	Originality	2.81	−.10	.04	1.08	1.12
	Complexity	2.96	−.66	.05	.92	.93
	Emotionality	2.17	1.19	.04	1.17	1.18
	Descriptiveness	2.95	−.43	.04	.85	.85
Title	Title 1	2.66	.15	.04	.98	.99
	Title 2	2.87	−.24	.05	1.02	.99
	Title 3	2.74	−.03	.04	.96	.99
	Title 4	2.63	.05	.05	1.08	1.08
	Title 5	2.70	.07	.05	1.04	1.06
Rater	Rater 1 (RUS/US)	2.57	.31	.03	1.00	1.01
	Rater 2 (RUS)	2.69	.30	.05	1.01	.99
	Rater 3 (RUS)	2.78	.16	.04	.98	1.03
	Rater 4 (US)	2.96	−.16	.06	1.01	1.00
	Rater 5 (US)	2.96	−.61	.06	1.01	1.08

The analysis of rater by country interaction suggested the absence of a significant DRF, $t_{(406)} = .05$, $p = .96$. Thus, the rater who was "linking" the U.S. and Russian samples applied the scoring rubrics consistently in the same fashion across the two samples. However, the analysis of DIF at the item level revealed significant item by country bias: out of the four items, two—Complexity and Emotionality—were differentially difficult for the two samples. Specifically, adjusting for the overall level of creativity and rater severity, it was more difficult for Russian students to obtain higher scores on Emotionality (item severity = 1.54), compared to the U.S. students (item severity = .80), $t_{(928)} = -8.06$, $p < .001$. On the other hand, Complexity was easier for Russian (−.72) compared to U.S. students (−.14), $t_{(909)} = 6.46$, $p < .001$.

Although the overall magnitude of bias in both cases was moderate, and differential item functioning in the two samples explained only .77% of the total variance in Creative Stories scores, it had important implications for the possible comparisons of the creativity scores in the two groups. Thus, without adjusting for bias, Russian students overall received higher creative ability estimates (Est. = .73, SE = .02) compared to the U.S. students (Est. = .59, SE = .04), for test of resulting ability estimates, the fixed all-same chi-square; χ^2 (1) = 8.60, $p < .01$ (Linacre, 2009). In order to examine whether these differences could be attributable to DIF, we reanalyzed the data while respecifying the rating scale structure in a way that permitted the two samples to have unique item difficulty estimates for Emotionality and Complexity. After the adjustment for bias, the two samples were no longer significantly different on the overall creative ability estimates, M = .51, SE =.02, and M = .51, SE = .04 for Russian and U.S. samples, respectively, χ^2 (1) = 0.05, $p = .96$.

Confirmatory Multigroup Factor Analysis. Using confirmatory factor analysis, we examined the cross-cultural invariance of the Creative Stories task by evaluating a set of multigroup models that imposed constraints on the overall structure of the model and patterns of item-factor loadings (configural invariance), magnitude of item-factor loadings (metric invariance), item intercept values (scalar invariance), and error variances (residual invariance). The baseline one-factor model (Figure 4.1) included four indicator variables that had loadings on the common factor of creative ability. One of the loadings has been set to 1 for the purpose of model identification and latent variable scaling. The model displayed satisfactory fit in the U.S. sample, χ^2 (2) = .11, $p = .943$, comparative fit index (CFI) = 1.00, Root Mean Square Error of Approximation (RMSEA) < .001, and, although somewhat worse, satisfactory fit in the Russian sample, χ^2 (2) = 9.86, $p = .007$, CFI = 0.96, RMSEA = 0.10. The two-sample configural invariance model displayed satisfactory fit, χ^2 (4) = 10.08, $p = .038$, CFI = 0.98, RMSEA = 0.08, suggesting that the configural invariance of the one-factor solution holds across both samples.

Figure 4.1. Factorial Structure (Based on CFA) of the Creative Stories Task in Russian and U.S. Students (Standardized Estimates)

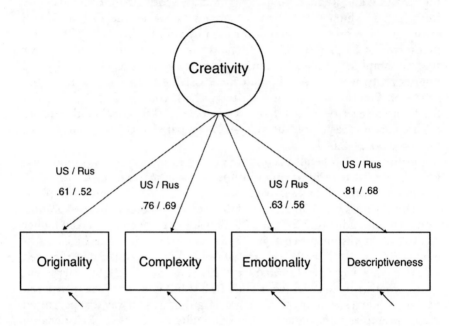

At the next step, we constrained the freely estimated item-factor loadings to be equal across the two groups: this metric invariance model displayed satisfactory fit (χ^2 (7) = 12.84, p = .076, CFI = 0.98, RMSEA = 0.06), and the difference between the levels of the fit of the configural and metric invariance models was not significant, ($\Delta\chi^2$ (3) = 2.76, p = .43, ΔCFI < 0.01). The examination of the results of the Lagrange Multiplier (LM) constraint testing statistic suggested that, across the two groups, the factor loadings were similar in magnitude, and all ps were >.05, indicating full metric invariance of the Creative Stories task in the samples of Russian and U.S. students.

To examine scalar invariance, in addition to imposing the set of constraints of the metric model, we constrained item intercepts to be equal in both groups of students. The model displayed worse fit, χ^2 (10) = 52.45, p < .001, CFI = 0.97, RMSEA = .080, than the metric invariance model, $\Delta\chi^2$ (3) = 39.61, p < .001, ΔCFI = 0.01. The examination of parameter estimates and results of LM testing suggested that the intercepts were noninvariant for the Emotionality item (at p < .001), corroborating the results from the MFRM analysis. Removing the constraint of item variance equality for Emotionality led to improved model fit, and the partial scalar invariance was reached, χ^2 (8) = 16.50, p = .036, CFI = 0.99, RMSEA = .059, $\Delta\chi^2$ (2) = 3.66, p = .16, ΔCFI < 0.01.

Finally, when we constrained item residuals to be equal in both groups, in addition to imposing the partial scalar invariance constraints, none of the items demonstrated noninvariant error variances, and the model displayed satisfactory fit, χ^2 (12) = 19.37, p = .08, CFI = 0.99, RMSEA = .041. This model showed a fit similar to that of the model with partial scalar invariance constraints only, $\Delta\chi^2$ (4) = 2.88 p = .58, ΔCFI < .01, suggesting that residual error invariance holds for the Creative Stories task.

Discussion

Using two different analytical approaches, we demonstrated the partial cross-cultural invariance of the Creative Stories task, an open-ended measure of verbal creativity that relied on ratings provided by multiple raters who scored creative stories on four different dimensions. Our many-facet Rasch analysis suggested that, despite higher within- compared to between-country levels of interrater reliability, the raters were able to apply the scoring rubrics consistently when scoring stories written by U.S. and Russian students. The analysis of differential item functioning, however, suggested that two items exhibited significant bias—it was more difficult for Russian students to obtain higher ratings on Emotionality, compared to the U.S. students, and the situation was reversed for Complexity. The results held when, in a follow-up analysis within a generalized linear model (GLM) framework, the linking bilingual expert was removed from the data. Although these biases explained only a minor fraction of the variance in students' creativity ratings, they were sufficient to drive the statistically significant difference in latent creativity estimates in the two samples. When adjusted for this bias, the group differences in overall creativity levels disappeared, suggesting that, overall, Russian and U.S. undergraduates display similar levels of verbal creativity in the written domain.

We obtained nearly identical results using multigroup confirmatory factor analysis for cross-cultural invariance testing. Thus, the measurement model was invariant in the two samples at the configural level and the metric level but was only partially invariant at the scalar and residual level. The partial scalar noninvariance was driven by the significant difference in the Emotionality item intercept between the two samples in the direction parallel to the findings from the MFRM analysis. Although the two methods differ in assumptions, properties, and interpretations of measurement invariance analyses, they converged on Emotionality as the particularly noninvariant element of the Creative Stories task. The advantage of the MFRM analysis is its ability to handle complex rater plans and take into account nonlinearity of the scores as manifested in category thresholds; the advantage of the CFA, on the other hand, is its ability to model differential item discrimination. The two approaches can be viewed as complementary and tend to produce similar results (Salzberger & Sinkovics, 2006), although the research on the comparative power of these approaches in detecting measurement noninvariance is scarce.

All other parameters held equal, Russian students tended to receive lower scores on Emotionality, a Creative Stories item that requires the raters to evaluate the presence and efficiency of the emotional component in written stories. Specifically, the raters were asked to evaluate whether the story mentioned emotional states and used mental language, the richness of these emotional representations, and whether the story was effective in eliciting an emotion from the raters. Emotions have long been recognized as at least partially culturally mediated despite showing substantial evidence for the presence of certain cross-cultural universals (Russell, 1991). Creative writing places heavy demands on the use of the symbolic system that might reflect the different ways in which different cultures label, conceptualize, and describe emotions—that is, language (Kovecses, 2003; Wierzbicka, 1986). This point of view has received substantial support in linguistic anthropology (Goddard & Zhengdao, 2014; Wilce, 2014) and suggests the need for a detailed semantic analysis of cross-cultural representations of emotions but also of the patterns of the use of language to describe mental states in general and emotions in particular. These patterns can be identified in both conversational discourse and writing (Edwards, 1999). In fact, they are likely more pronounced and institutionalized in writing because the latter is a cornerstone of the transmission of cultural knowledge and one of its key communicative channels.

In our study, the raters scored the use of emotional language rather than performed a semantic analysis of the emotion representations in Russian or English. Why would Russian students score lower specifically on Emotionality? Pending the detailed semantic analysis of the emotional descriptors in English and Russian used by the students in our sample, we would like to suggest that these findings might reflect the bias originating from the interaction between task demands (i.e., creative writing under a time limit) and the patterns of use of emotional language specific to each culture and language. Although both Russian and English have emotion nouns, adjectives, pseudoparticiples, and (in)transitive verbs, the distribution of emotion terms across these categories differs significantly (e.g., Russian has more intransitive verbs than English does). In addition to these distributional differences, Russian speakers display a pattern of use of emotion words that is slightly different from that of English speakers—that is, Russian speakers favor intransitive and reflexive emotion verbs, and English speakers prefer emotion adjectives; this difference has been suggested to originate from the conceptualization of emotion as a more voluntary inner activity in Russian but as more of a reactive state in English (Wierzbicka, 1998). A corpus study by Pavlenko and Driagina (2007) partially corroborated this differentiation of verbal versus adjectival pattern of use of mental lexicon. Thus, one of the possible explanations for our findings is that Russian students used less of the mental lexicon given

NEW DIRECTIONS FOR CHILD AND ADOLESCENT DEVELOPMENT • DOI: 10.1002/cad

the limited time resources: in this case, emotion verbs would be used less frequently to save "space" for action verbs that have a greater potential for propelling the story plot, thereby reducing the overall use of emotion words.

Our tentative explanation for the pattern of results obtained in this study can be tested empirically through further detailed lexical-semantic and frequency analysis of the stories written by the students in our sample. Yet, we would also like to acknowledge that there exist several other potential sources of variance (or, for that matter, lack of invariance) that we did not examine. These include, but are not limited to, students' gender, age, academic major and area of concentration, academic achievement, and adaptation to college life, as well as the interactions among them and between them and other unidentified factors that mediate the effects of culture on creative cognition and behavior. We also found that Russian students tended to receive higher ratings on Complexity, a measure of the elaboration and complexity of their creative writing. This is not surprising given the heavy emphasis on composition in the standard Russian language and literature curriculum but could also reflect the selective nature of the studied population (Kornilova, Kornilov, & Chumakova, 2009).

As pointed out by the anonymous reviewer, the results of this study are interpreted as indicating partial cross-cultural invariance of creativity as measured with Creative Stories. Within this approach, expert ratings are viewed as indicators of creativity, and the results of the analysis suggest that while the application of the rating scores seems to be consistent in two samples, they are partially locally biased, favoring the U.S. sample. We would like to note that such a bias could indeed reflect cultural bias in expert ratings rather than be driven by the culturally moderated properties of the product (i.e., the story) itself. Interestingly, Emotionality was the dimension of creativity for which the lowest between-country reliability estimates were obtained, suggesting that the same stories were somewhat differently rated by the Russian compared to the U.S. raters. A follow-up analysis performed in the GLM framework suggested that even excluding the linking bilingual rater and regressing out scores on three other dimensions did not eliminate the group difference in Emotionality estimates between the two samples; this suggests that the Russian students consistently received lower scores on the Emotionality item. This bias could be also driven by culturally mediated conceptions of emotion and the role of emotionality in creativity, a possibility that should be explored in future studies of implicit conceptions of creativity and creative writing in Russian.

The results obtained in this study suggest that creative writing can be at least partially considered as culturally invariant, thereby indicating the commonalities in the overall architecture of cognitive processes that contribute to creativity in the written domain. Yet, we identified a dimension of creative writing, namely, emotionality, that seems to be particularly susceptible to cultural influences, necessitating further research into the connection between the use of mental lexicon, imagination, and verbal creativity across cultures. Such an examination is necessary for the field to bridge the gap between its methodological and conceptual approaches to creativity. As mentioned in the beginning of this paper, culture guides the development of creativity and patterns of its manifestation; yet, it also serves as the key contextual element for the evaluation of creative products. The increasing globalization of the world poses new challenges for the field, particularly related to the issues of cultural specificity and cultural universality of creative cognition and the methods used to measure it and also to the issues of multiculturality and the blurring of cultural boundaries (for a review, see Mourgues et al., 2014) and its implications for our understanding of the very concept of culture and "cross-cultural" differences or similarities. Our study illustrates one of the possible methodological frameworks for addressing these issues by linking the properties of a measurement instrument with those of the linguistic and cultural systems that shape creativity and the way it manifests in specific creative products evaluated with that particular instrument.

Acknowledgments

This research and the preparation of this manuscript was supported by the College Board and the Russian Foundation for Humanities (RGNF), project No. 13-06-00049.

References

Bentler, P. M. (1995). *EQS structural equations program manual*. Encino, CA: Multivariate Software.

Bond, T. G., & Fox, C. M. (2007). *Applying the Rasch Model: Fundamental measurement in the human sciences* (2nd ed.). Mahwah, NJ: Lawrence Erlbaum.

Byrne, B. M. (2006). *Structural equation modeling with EQS*. Mahwah, NJ: Lawrence Erlbaum.

Cohen, J. (1960). A coefficient of agreement for nominal scales. *Educational and Psychological Measurement, 20*, 37–46.

Edwards, D. (1999). Emotion discourse. *Culture & Psychology, 5*, 271–291.

Erez, M., & Nouri, R. (2010). Creativity: The influence of cultural, social, and work contexts. *Management and Organization Review, 6*(3), 351–370.

Goddard, C., & Zhengdao, Y. (2014). Exploring "happiness" and "pain" across languages and cultures. *International Journal of Language and Culture, 18*, 131–148.

Kornilov, S. A., & Grigorenko, E. L. (2010). Методический комплекс для диагностики академических, творческих и практических способностей [Metodičeskij kompleks dlja diagnostiki akademičeskih atvorčeskih i praktičeskih sposobnostej]. *Psihologičeskij žurnal [Психологический журнал], 31*(2), 90–103.

Kornilova, T. V., Kornilov, S. A., & Chumakova, M. A. (2009). Subjective evaluations of intelligence and academic self-concept predict academic achievement: Evidence from a selective student population. *Learning and Individual Differences, 19*(4), 596–608.

Kovecses, Z. (2003). *Metaphor and emotion*. Cambridge, MA: Cambridge University Press.

Kroeber, A. L., & Kluckhon, C. (1952). *Culture: A critical review of concepts and definitions*. Cambridge, MA: Peabody Museum.

Landis, J. R., & Koch, G. G. (1977). The measurement of observer agreement for categorical data. *Biometrics*, 33(1), 159–174.

Linacre, J. M. (1997). KR-20/Cronbach Alpha or Rasch Person Reliability: Which tells the "truth"? *Rasch Measurement Transactions*, 11(3), 580–581.

Linacre, J. M. (2009). Facets Rasch measurement computer program (Version 3.65.0). Chicago: WINSTEPS.com.

Lubart, T. (2010). Cross-cultural perspectives on creativity. In J. C. Kaufman & R. J. Sternberg (Eds.), *The Cambridge handbook of creativity* (pp. 265–278). Cambridge, MA: Cambridge University Press.

Mourgues, C., Barbot, B., Tan, M., & Grigorenko, E. L. (2014). The interaction between culture and the development of creativity. In L. A. Jensen (Ed.), *The Oxford handbook of human development and culture: An interdisciplinary perspective*. Oxford: Oxford University Press.

Pavlenko, A., & Driagina, V. (2007). Russian emotion vocabulary in American learners' narratives. *Modern Language Journal*, 91(2), 213–234.

Rubera, G., Ordanini, A., & Griffith, D. A. (2011). Incorporating cultural values for understanding the influence of perceived product creativity on intention to buy: An examination in Italy and the US. *Journal of International Business Studies*, 42, 459–476.

Runco, M. A., & Jaeger, G. J. (2012). The standard definition of creativity. *Creativity Research Journal*, 24(1), 92–96.

Russell, J. A. (1991). Culture and categorization of emotions. *Psychological Bulletin*, 110(3), 426–450.

Salzberger, T., & Sinkovics, R. R. (2006). Reconsidering the problem of data equivalence in international marketing research. *International Marketing Review*, 23(4), 390–417.

Sternberg, R. J. (2012). The assessment of creativity: An investment-based approach. *Creativity Research Journal*, 24(1), 3–12.

Sternberg, R. J., Grigorenko, E. L., Hart, L., Jarvin, L., Kwiatkowski, J., Newman, T., et al. (2007). *Transitions in the development of giftedness* (RM07230). Storrs: University of Connecticut, National Research Center on the Gifted and Talented.

Sternberg, R. J., & Lubart, T. (1995). *Defying the crowd: Cultivating creativity in a culture of conformity*. New York: Free Press.

Wierzbicka, A. (1986). Human emotions: Universal or culture-specific? *American Anthropologist*, 88(3), 584–594.

Wierzbicka, A. (1998). Russian emotional expression. *Ethos*, 26, 456–483.

Wilce, J. M. (2014). Current emotion research in linguistic anthropology. *Emotion Review*, 6, 77.

Wright, B. D., & Masters, G. N. (1990). Computation of OUTFIT and INFIT statistics. *Rasch Measurement Transactions*, 3(4), 84–85.

SERGEY A. KORNILOV *is a postdoctoral associate at Yale University. He received his PhD in experimental psychology from University of Connecticut.*

TATIANA V. KORNILOVA *is a professor of general psychology at Moscow State University, Moscow, Russian Federation. She received her PhD and completed requirements for habilitation at Moscow State University.*

ELENA L. GRIGORENKO *is Emily Fraser Beede professor at Yale University. She received her PhD in psychology from Moscow State University and PhD in developmental psychology and genetics from Yale University.*

Cassotti, M., Agogué, M., Camarda, A., Houdé, O., & Borst, G. (2016). Inhibitory control as a core process of creative problem solving and idea generation from childhood to adulthood. In B. Barbot (Ed.), *Perspectives on creativity development. New Directions for Child and Adolescent Development, 151,* 61–72.

Inhibitory Control as a Core Process of Creative Problem Solving and Idea Generation from Childhood to Adulthood

Mathieu Cassotti, Marine Agogué, Anaëlle Camarda, Olivier Houdé, Grégoire Borst

Abstract

Developmental cognitive neuroscience studies tend to show that the prefrontal brain regions (known to be involved in inhibitory control) are activated during the generation of creative ideas. In the present article, we discuss how a dual-process model of creativity—much like the ones proposed to account for decision making and reasoning—could broaden our understanding of the processes involved in creative ideas generation. When generating creative ideas, children, adolescents, and adults tend to follow "the path of least resistance" and propose solutions that are built on the most common and accessible knowledge within a specific domain, leading to fixation effect. In line with recent theory of typical cognitive development, we argue that the ability to resist the spontaneous activation of design heuristics, to privilege other types of reasoning, might be critical to generate creative ideas at all ages. In the present review, we demonstrate that inhibitory control at all ages can actually support creativity. Indeed, the ability to think of something truly new and original requires first inhibiting spontaneous solutions that come to mind quickly and unconsciously and then exploring new ideas using a generative type of reasoning. © 2016 Wiley Periodicals, Inc.

The ability to inhibit prepotent associations or previous and inappropriate ideas seems to be a critical process to generate new ideas and creative solutions to problems (Dietrich & Kanso, 2010). Although considerable efforts in the field of developmental psychology and neuroscience have been devoted to identifying the role of inhibitory control in reasoning and decision making (Crone & Dahl, 2012; Houdé & Borst, 2014, 2015), there are to date few studies that have examined whether this executive function may facilitate creative ideation at all ages (Kleibeuker, Koolschijn, Jolles, De Dreu, & Crone, 2013a). This relative lack of interest is partly because of how these two fields define inhibition. Indeed, many studies in the field of creativity considered inhibition as a social process hindering creativity (Kohn & Smith, 2011). According to this view, social pressure, evaluation, and conformity would lead individuals to inhibit their creative potential (Amabile, Goldfarb, & Brackfleld, 1990). Even if social inhibition is undoubtedly a fundamental aspect of creative thinking, this concept differs from the process of inhibition at the core of recent theories of typical cognitive development (Diamond & Lee, 2011). In these models, inhibition, and more specifically inhibitory control, is viewed as a basic process enabling the suppression of prepotent but irrelevant response tendencies and previously acquired knowledge (Houdé & Borst, 2014, 2015). In this article, we discuss how developmental models that emphasize the role of inhibitory control in overcoming reasoning and decision-making biases could broaden our understanding of the processes involved in creative problem solving and idea generation. Specifically, we examine whether the ability to think of something truly new (i.e., original, unexpected) and appropriate (i.e., useful, adaptive concerning task constraints, see Sternberg & Lubart, 1996) requires first inhibiting easy solutions that spontaneously come to mind and then generating creative ideas.

Dual Process Theory and Reasoning-Biases Inhibition

Consider the following example:

> In a lake, there is a patch of lily pads. Every day, the patch doubles in size.

> If it takes 48 days for the patch to cover the entire lake, how long would it take for the patch to cover half of the lake? _____ days

When trying to answer this problem, an intuitive response spontaneously comes to mind: 24 days (Frederick, 2005). It is true that most of the time to get half a set, the most basic solution is to divide it by two. However, this response that immediately jumps to mind is false! Indeed, we tend to ignore a fundamental and explicitly mentioned part of the problem, which is that every day, the patch doubles in size. Thus, the correct response is "47 days" because the patch of lily pads will cover half of the lake surface

NEW DIRECTIONS FOR CHILD AND ADOLESCENT DEVELOPMENT • DOI: 10.1002/cad

Figure 5.1. Schematic representation of the dual process models (see Houdé & Borst, 2014)

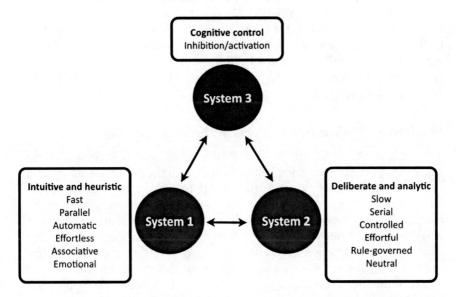

on the 47th day, and doubling it overnight will cover the full surface the 48th day. To explain such reasoning biases, authors have postulated the existence of two distinct system of thinking (De Neys, Rossi, & Houdé, 2013; Houdé, 1997; Kahneman, 2011). Dual system theories generally oppose an intuitive-heuristic system (named System 1) to a deliberate-analytic system (named System 2). System 1 operations are typically effortless, rapid, global, or holistic, and often emotionally charged. System 2, in contrast, is slow, controlled, serial, effortful, and involves cognitively costly strategies (see Figure 5.1). Consequently, these dual theories predict qualitatively different judgments and decisions depending on which system is running.

According to this theoretical framework, cognitive biases evidenced in children, adolescents, and adults are not due to a lack of logical skills *per se*, but result from a specific failure to inhibit intuitive responses generated automatically by System 1. Thus, to solve reasoning problems such as "the patch of lily pads" problem, one must first inhibit (System 3) the misleading heuristic belonging to System 1, and then activate the logical algorithm of System 2.

From a developmental perspective, studies converged in showing that an increasing number of heuristics are acquired over the course of development that are used with increasing frequency (De Neys & Vanderputte, 2011; Houdé & Borst, 2014; Reyna, Wilhelms, McCormick, & Weldon, 2015). With the respective development of the intuitive-heuristic System 1 and the deliberative-analytic System 2, the experiences of conflict and

NEW DIRECTIONS FOR CHILD AND ADOLESCENT DEVELOPMENT • DOI: 10.1002/cad

inhibitory control demand may change with age. In addition, several lines of evidence suggest that the ability to inhibit the misleading intuitive strategies improves from childhood to late adolescence (De Neys & Van Gelder, 2009; Houdé & Borst, 2014, 2015). Unlike other traditional models of cognitive development such as the Piagetian model, these dual-process models, by focusing not only on the development of the two systems but also on the development of inhibitory control abilities, can account for nonlinear patterns of development observed in reasoning and decision making (Houdé & Borst, 2014, 2015).

Fixation and Inhibition in Creative Problem Solving

Much like researchers in the field of reasoning seeking to understand what causes one to fail to reason logically, researchers in the field of creativity seek to determine the factors leading one to fail to provide original ideas or problem solutions. For instance, numerous studies have reported that creative problem-solving capabilities can be blocked by mental fixation (Storm & Angello, 2010). These studies stress how previous knowledge or ideas can constrain the generation of alternative solutions during creative problem solving. One of the most striking examples of this creativity failure is the so-called functional fixedness phenomenon, initially described by Duncker (1945). For instance, in the "candle problem" (Adamson, 1952; German & Barrett, 2005), participants are presented with a tabletop containing a book of matches, a box of tacks, and a candle. They are asked to find a way to fix and light the candle on the wall in such a way that it will burn without dripping wax onto the table below.

This problem is difficult to solve because people are fixed on the traditional function of the box as a container. Indeed, the optimal solution requires emptying the box of tacks to use it in an unfamiliar way such as a platform. Frequently, adults fail to easily find this solution when the box is presented as being full of tacks because they remain focused on the typical function of the box.

Within the context of dual-process models, functional fixedness may arise from an intuitively-generated mental representation of the classical use of the object belonging to System 1. Therefore, inhibitory control may allow the suppression of this first intuitive response in order to consider alternative uses of the objects. Although no study has demonstrated a direct relationship between inhibitory control and creative performance in the candle problem, there is increasing evidence that the ability to overcome fixation in various problem-solving situations require inhibitory control (Dietrich & Kanso, 2010; Storm & Angello, 2010; Storm & Patel, 2014). Indeed, studies in adults clearly demonstrated that higher level of inhibitory control is associated with greater success on creative problems solving tasks involving mental fixation (Storm & Angello, 2010). Additional empirical evidences in favor of the hypothesis that inhibitory control is a core component of creative problem solving came from a developmental neuroimaging study in adolescent and adults (Kleibeuker et al., 2013b). Greater activation of the inferior frontal gyrus and the dorsolateral prefrontal cortex, two brain regions classically associated with executive functions and inhibitory control in particular, were observed when participants provided optimal solutions to the problems. In addition, these two brain structures were more activated in adolescents than in adults, suggesting that the maturation of the prefrontal cortex regions sustaining inhibitory-control ability is still developing during adolescence in agreement with the protracted development of these prefrontal regions until early adulthood (Giedd et al., 2009).

Developmental studies of functional fixedness have reported, surprisingly, that 5- and 6-year-old children seem immune to this cognitive bias as opposed to older children and adults (Defeyter & German, 2003; German & Barrett, 2005; German & Defeyter, 2000). Indeed, using a child-friendly adaptation of the candle problem, German and Defeyter (2000) clearly demonstrated that young children are not fixed on the typical function of the object, allowing them to solve the problem more easily than older children. This finding makes sense in light of dual-process models of cognitive development according to which heuristics belonging to System 1 progressively emerge during the course of childhood (Houdé & Borst, 2014). This result is also consistent with results in decision-making studies showing that young children are less susceptible to various cognitive biases (Reyna, Wilhelms, McCormick, & Weldon, 2015). Whereas overcoming functional fixedness in older children and adults requires inhibitory control, younger children might not need inhibitory control to generate alternative function of objects because the classical functions of the object might not be as strong as in adolescents and adults. In other words, children might not need inhibitory control in these contexts to be creative simply because, unlike adolescents and adults, they experience a lower functional fixedness (or at least a different type of fixation) in creative problem solving.

Fixation and Inhibition in Creative Ideas Generation

Although reasoning and creative problem-solving studies suggest that inhibitory control is involved in overcoming cognitive biases and mental fixation, one could wonder whether this process is also fundamental in circumstances where individuals cannot simply choose between existing strategies but must propose a variety of new strategies (DeHaan, 2011). Just as in other contexts, it seems that individuals face numerous cognitive biases when asked to generate creative ideas (Finke, Ward, & Smith, 1992; Ward, Patterson, & Sifonis, 2004). Indeed, people tend to follow "the path of least resistance" and propose solutions that are built on the most common and accessible knowledge within a specific domain (Agogué et al., 2014; Smith, Ward, & Finke, 1995). For example, when individuals must imagine and draw an animal that lives on another planet very different from

Earth, a number of typical examples of animals living on Earth spontaneously jump to mind (Abraham & Windmann, 2007). These intuitive and spontaneous representations of what classically constitute animals on Earth (bilateral symmetry of the shape, presence of common appendage or sense organs) impede the creative process, leading to fixation effect in both children and adults (Cacciari, Levorato, & Cicogna, 1997). According to the dual-process view and in line with the "path of least resistance" model (Ward et al., 2004), the difficulty of generating creative ideas might result from a specific failure to inhibit intuitive responses leading to fixation effect generated automatically by System 1. Thus, to provide original ideas in a problem such as "the alien drawing task," one must first inhibit the intuitive representations of what classically constitute animals on Earth (representations belonging to System 1) and then activate conceptual expansion reasoning (in System 2).

Interestingly, the results of a recent study suggest that the nature of fixation effect during the generation of creative ideas may develop with age, education, and expertise (Agogué, Poirel, Pineau, Houdé, & Cassotti, 2014). Using a creative idea generation task that involves designing a method to drop a hen's egg from a height of 10 meters (32 feet) to ensure that it does not break (called "the egg task"), the authors found that the fixation effect of children diverges qualitatively from that of adults. Indeed, most of the responses proposed by the adults were based on spontaneously activated knowledge and consisted of using an inert device to dampen the shock, protect the egg, or slow the fall (e.g., to slow the fall with a parachute). On the contrary, more original solutions that consisted of using a living device or of modifying the natural properties of the egg (e.g., training a bird to catch the egg during the fall or freezing the egg before dropping it) were less often provided by the participants. Although 10-year-old children were also fixed on solutions that consisted of protecting the egg or dampening the shock, they did not spontaneously propose to slow the fall using, for example, a parachute. In line with dual-process models, these results suggest that the design heuristics belonging to System 1 used by participants to explore the potential solutions to the task and leading to fixation differed between children and adults, although children knew what parachutes were and how parachutes worked. Moreover, a recent study on industrial designer with the same egg task provided indirect evidence that inhibitory control might be involved in the ability to overcome fixation effect during creative ideas generation (Agogué, Le Masson, Dalmasso, Houdé, & Cassotti, 2015). The authors found that industrial designers outperformed engineers with regard to fluency and originality, and gave more solutions outside of the fixation effect in the egg task. It was argued that industrial designers outperformed engineers because they were more efficient at inhibiting fixation effect. This assumption is in line with results of a previous study showing that industrial designers exhibited higher scores of creativity assessed with the Torrance Tests of Creative Thinking and showed higher inhibitory control

NEW DIRECTIONS FOR CHILD AND ADOLESCENT DEVELOPMENT • DOI: 10.1002/cad

skills as indicated by the absence of a Stroop interference effect (i.e., a classical inhibitory control task) compared to a control group. In addition, the creative abilities of industrial designers were positively associated with their performance on the Stroop task (Edl, Benedek, Papousek, Weiss, & Fink, 2014).

Additional evidence for the role of inhibitory control and flexible cognitive control in creative ideas generation has been provided by a series of studies showing positive correlations between inhibition measures and divergent thinking performance in adults (Beaty, Silvia, Nusbaum, Jauk, & Benedek, 2014; Benedek, Franz, Heene, & Neubauer, 2012; Vartanian, 2009; Zabelina & Robinson, 2010). Moreover, neuroimaging studies have consistently reported a relationship between the ability to generate highly creative responses and activations in specific prefrontal brain regions known to be implicated in executive functions (Benedek et al., 2014; Dietrich & Kanso, 2010). More specifically, verbal and visuospatial creativity elicited activations in the anterior cingulate cortex, the inferior frontal gyri, and the middle frontal gyri, suggesting that conflict monitoring, inhibitory control, and working memory might be important for creativity (Boccia, Piccardi, Palermo, Nori, & Palmiero, 2015). Critically, a recent neuroimaging study demonstrated that brain activation in the inferior frontal gyrus—a brain region known to be implicated in inhibitory control (Houdé, Rossi, Lubin, & Joliot, 2010)—is positively related to originality and appropriateness aspects of divergent thinking (Benedek et al., 2014). Studies showing that more creative adults have better inhibitory control efficiency and recruit to a greater extent brain regions involved in inhibitory control than less creative adults are in agreement with the prediction of our dual-process model of creativity that creative idea generation requires the inhibition of dominant and common ideas belonging to System 1 to explore new concepts using a generative type of reasoning (conceptual expansion or analogical reasoning).

Despite these recent findings on adults, there are few developmental studies on the relationship between inhibitory control and creative idea generation in children and adolescents. To the best of our knowledge, only one developmental neuroimaging study has directly tested the involvement of inhibitory control brain regions in divergent thinking in a developmental perspective (Kleibeuker et al., 2013a). In this elegant study, the authors investigated the neural correlates of multiple creative ideas generation in both adolescents and adults. Using an alternative uses task in which participants were requested to generate alternative uses for conventional everyday objects such as a brick, they reported that brain activations in the left lateral prefrontal cortex regions supporting inhibitory control process were less activated in adolescent than in adults. Consistent with dual-process models postulating that inhibitory control is still developing during adolescent, these findings suggest that adolescent may be less effective to execute inhibitory control on intuitively generated solutions based on the typical function of the objects in the alternative uses task (i.e., fixation effect belonging to the intuitive System 1) compared to adults.

Limitations

In the present review, we have discussed how a dual-process model of creativity—much like the ones proposed for reasoning and decision making—may lead to significant progress in the understanding of the processes involved in creative cognition. Nevertheless, a few limitations of the present study should be acknowledged. First of all, because creativity is a complex phenomenon, different factors such as personality traits, emotional context, and social influences are known to highly contribute to creative performance. Although our model provides a basis for studying the development of creativity, and more specifically here, creative behaviors that include creative problem solving and creative ideas generation, further researches are necessary to determine how these critical factors modulate the activation of each system and the interactions between them.

The role of inhibitory control in creative ideas generation has been evidenced with verbal divergent thinking studies but few studies have investigated whether inhibitory control is also required to be creative in other domains such as in visuospatial or artistic creativity. The results of a meta-analysis of neuroimaging studies of creativity in three different domains including musical, verbal, and visuospatial (Boccia et al., 2015) suggest that verbal and visuospatial creativity, but not musical creativity, rely on the activation of a network of executive brain regions including inhibitory control ones. Thus, inhibitory control might be required to be creative only in the verbal and visuospatial domains.

Finally, although neuroimaging and behavioral studies converge in showing that better inhibitory control leads to higher creativity, some studies have reported that poorer inhibitory ability can facilitate creative performance (Radel, Davranche, Fournier, & Dietrich, 2015). For example, using noninvasive brain stimulation, Mayseless and Shamay-Tsoory (2015) reported that decreasing the activity in the left frontal parts of the brain and increasing activity in the right frontal parts of the brain—a brain modulation supposed to reduce cognitive control—have a positive effect on creative ideas production. In sharp contrast with this finding, another noninvasive brain stimulation study reported that a hyperactivation of the prefrontal cortex was beneficial for creative production, suggesting that better cognitive control led to better creative ideas generation (Colombo, Bartesaghi, Simonelli, & Antonietti, 2015). In a similar vein, numerous studies on clinical disorders associated with inhibitory control deficits suggest that impaired cognitive control might facilitate original associations and stimulate creative ideas generation (see de Souza et al., 2014). We note, however, that these patients rarely exhibited specific deficits in inhibitory control. Thus, to account for the discrepancies in the literature regarding the role of creativity, future researches should explore the respective contribution of latent inhibition, social inhibition, and cognitive inhibition to creativity.

Conclusion

Taken together, the behavioral and neuroimaging data reviewed in this article converge in showing that the development of creative problem solving and idea generation relies not only on the ability to make intuitive associations but also on the ability to suppress (inhibit) previously acquired knowledge or prepotent irrelevant classical solutions.

In contrast to the assumption that reduced inhibitory control may foster remote associations and stimulate creativity (Radel et al., 2015), we have reported numerous evidence in the literature that the ability to resist (inhibit) intuitive-heuristic reasoning leading to fixation is critical to generate creative solutions to problems at all ages by allowing one to adopt other types of reasoning (e.g., analogical thinking and conceptual expansion) belonging to System 2.

Although an increasing number of studies in adults focus on the role of inhibitory control in creative thinking (Beaty et al., 2014; Benedek et al., 2012, 2014; Dietrich & Kanso, 2010; Storm & Angello, 2010), there are still many challenges to be addressed to fully understand the processes that enable to break conventional or obvious patterns of thinking in a developmental perspective of creative ideas generation. Indeed, more research is required to clarify the relationship between creativity and the developmental trajectories of fixation effects (System 1), generative-type of reasoning (System 2), and inhibitory control (System 3). This new line of developmental research should also clarify the interactions between these systems to determine whether System 1 and System 2 are activated serially or in parallel (De Neys et al., 2013). Finally, given that previous developmental studies demonstrated that inhibitory control can be improved (Diamond & Lee, 2011), studies should investigate whether interventions based on training inhibitory control can help children, adolescents, and adults overcome fixation effects during creative problem solving and idea generation.

Acknowledgment

This research was financed by a grant from the French National Research Agency (ANR IDéfixE).

References

Abraham, A., & Windmann, S. (2007). Creative cognition: The diverse operations and the prospect of applying a cognitive neuroscience perspective. *Methods*, 42, 38–48.

Adamson, R. E. (1952). Functional fixedness as related to problem solving: a repetition of three experiments. *Journal of Experimental Psychology*, 44(4), 288–291.

Agogué, M., Kazakçi, A., Hatchuel, A., Masson, P., Weil, B., Poirel, N., et al. (2014). The impact of type of examples on originality: Explaining fixation and stimulation effects. *Journal of Creative Behavior, 48*(1), 1–12.

Agogué, M., Le Masson, P., Dalmasso, C., Houdé, O., & Cassotti, M. (2015). Resisting classical solutions: The creative mind of industrial designers and engineers. *Psychology of Aesthetics, Creativity, and the Arts, 9*(3), 313–318.

Agogué, M., Poirel, N., Pineau, A., Houdé, O., & Cassotti, M. (2014). The impact of age and training on creativity: A design-theory approach to study fixation effects. *Thinking Skills and Creativity, 11*, 33–41.

Amabile, T. M., Goldfarb, P., & Brackfleld, S. C. (1990). Social influences on creativity: Evaluation, coaction, and surveillance. *Creativity Research Journal, 3*(1), 6–21.

Beaty, R. E., Silvia, P. J., Nusbaum, E. C., Jauk, E., & Benedek, M. (2014). The role of associative and executive processes in creative cognition. *Memory & Cognition, 42*(7), 1186–1197.

Benedek, M., Franz, F., Heene, M., & Neubauer, A. C. (2012). Differential effects of cognitive inhibition and intelligence on creativity. *Personality and Individual Differences, 53*, 480–485.

Benedek, M., Jauk, E., Fink, A., Koschutnig, K., Reishofer, G., Ebner, F., et al. (2014). To create or to recall? Neural mechanisms underlying the generation of creative new ideas. *NeuroImage, 88*, 125–133.

Boccia, M., Piccardi, L., Palermo, L., Nori, R., & Palmiero, M. (2015) Where do bright ideas occur in our brain? Meta-analytic evidence from neuroimaging studies of domain-specific creativity. *Frontiers in Psychology, 6*, 1195.

Cacciari, C., Levorato. M. C., & Cicogna, P. (1997). Imagination at work: Conceptual and linguistic creativity in children. In T. B. Ward, S. M. Smith, & J. Vaid, *Creative thought: An investigation of conceptual structures and processes* (pp. 145–177). Washington, DC: American Psychological Association.

Colombo, B., Bartesaghi, N., Simonelli, L., & Antonietti, A. (2015). The combined effects of neurostimulation and priming on creative thinking. A preliminary tDCS study on dorsolateral prefrontal cortex. *Frontiers in Human Neuroscience, 9*. doi: 10.3389/fnhum.2015.00403

Crone, E. A., & Dahl, R. E. (2012). Understanding adolescence as a period of social–affective engagement and goal flexibility. *Nature Reviews Neuroscience, 13*(9), 636–650.

Defeyter, M. A., & German, T. P. (2003). Acquiring an understanding of design: Evidence from children's insight problem solving. *Cognition, 89*, 133–155.

DeHaan, R. J. (2011). Teaching creative science thinking. *Science, 334*, 1499–1500.

De Neys, W., Rossi, S., and Houdé, O. (2013). Bats, balls and substitution sensitivity. *Psychonomic Bulletin & Review, 20*, 269–273.

De Neys, W., & Vanderputte, K. (2011). When less is not always more: Stereotype knowledge and reasoning development. *Developmental Psychology, 47*, 432–441.

De Neys, W., & Van Gelder, E. (2009). Logic and belief across the life span: the rise and fall of belief inhibition during syllogistic reasoning. *Developmental Science, 12*, 123–130.

de Souza, L. C., Guimarães, H. C., Teixeira, A. L., Caramelli, P., Levy, R., Dubois, B., et al. (2014). Frontal lobe neurology and the creative mind. *Frontiers in Psychology, 5*. doi: 10.3389/fpsyg.2014.00761

Diamond, A., & Lee, K. (2011). Interventions shown to aid executive function development in children 4 to 12 years old. *Science, 333*(6045), 959–964.

Dietrich, A., & Kanso, R. (2010). A review of EEG, ERP, and neuroimaging studies of creativity and insight. *Psychological Bulletin, 136*(5), 822–848.

Duncker, K. (1945). On problem-solving. *Psychological Monographs, 58*(5), 1–113.

Edl, S., Benedek, M., Papousek, I., Weiss, E. M., & Fink, A. (2014). Creativity and the stroop interference effect. *Personality and Individual Differences, 69*, 38–42.

Finke, R. A., Ward, T. B., & Smith, S. M. (1992). *Creative cognition: Theory, research, and applications.* Cambridge, MA: MIT Press.

Frederick, S. (2005). Cognitive reflection and decision making. *Journal of Economic Perspectives, 19*(4), 25–42.

German, T. P., & Barrett, H. C. (2005). Functional fixedness in a technologically sparse culture. *Psychological Science, 16*, 1–5.

German, T. P., & Defeyter, M. A. (2000). Immunity to functional fixedness in young children. *Psychonomic Bulletin & Review, 7*(4), 707–712.

Giedd, J. N., Lalonde, F. M., Celano, M. J., White, S. L., Wallace, G. L., Lee, N. R., & Lenroot, R. K. (2009). Anatomical brain magnetic resonance imaging of typically developing children and adolescents. *Journal of the American Academy of Child and Adolescent Psychiatry, 48*, 465–470.

Houdé, O. (1997). The problem of deductive competence and the inhibitory control of cognition. *Cahiers de Psychologie Cognitive/Current Psychology of Cognition, 16*, 108–113.

Houdé, O., & Borst, G. (2014). Measuring inhibitory control in children and adults. *Frontiers in Psychology, 5*, 616.

Houdé, O., & Borst, G. (2015) Evidence for an inhibitory-control theory of the reasoning brain. *Frontiers in Human Neuroscience, 9*, 148.

Houdé, O., Rossi, S., Lubin, A., & Joliot, M. (2010). Mapping numerical processing, reading, and executive functions in the developing brain: An fMRI meta-analysis of 52 studies including 842 children. *Developmental Science, 13*(6), 876–885.

Kahneman, D. (2011) *Thinking fast and slow.* New York : Farrar, Straus and Giroux.

Kleibeuker, S. W., Koolschijn, P. C. M. P., Jolles, D. D., De Dreu, C. K. W., & Crone, E. A. (2013a). The neural coding of creative idea generation across adolescence and early adulthood. *Frontiers in Human Neuroscience, 7*, 1–12.

Kleibeuker, S. W., Koolschijn, P. C. M. P., Jolles, D. D., Schel, M. A., De Dreu, C. K. W., & Crone, E. A. (2013b). Prefrontal cortex involvement in creative problem solving in middle adolescence and adulthood. *Developmental Cognitive Neuroscience, 5*, 197–206.

Kohn, N. W., & Smith, S. M. (2011). Collaborative fixation: Effects of others' ideas on brainstorming. *Applied Cognitive Psychology, 25*(3), 359–371.

Mayseless, N., & Shamay-Tsoory, S. G. (2015). Enhancing verbal creativity: Modulating creativity by altering the balance between right and left inferior frontal gyrus with tDCS. *Neuroscience, 291*, 167–176.

Radel, R., Davranche, K., Fournier, M., & Dietrich, A. (2015). The role of (dis) inhibition in creativity: Decreased inhibition improves idea generation. *Cognition, 134*, 110–120.

Reyna, V. F., Wilhelms, E. A., McCormick, M. J., & Weldon, R. B. (2015), Development of risky decision making: Fuzzy-trace theory and neurobiological perspectives. *Child Development Perspectives, 9*, 122–127.

Smith, S. M., Ward, T. B., & Finke, R. A. (1995). *The creative cognition approach.* Cambridge, MA: MIT Press.

Sternberg, R. J., & Lubart, T. I. (1996). Investing in creativity. *American Psychologist, 51*(7), 677.

Storm, B. C., & Angello, G. (2010). Overcoming fixation: Creative problem solving and retrieval-induced forgetting. *Psychological Science, 21*, 1263–1265.

Storm, B. C., & Patel, T. N. (2014). Forgetting as a consequence and enabler of creative thinking. *Journal of Experimental Psychology: Learning, Memory, and Cognition, 40*, 1594–1609.

Vartanian, O. (2009). Variable attention facilitates creative problem solving. *Psychology of Aesthetics, Creativity, and the Arts, 3*, 57–59.

Ward, T. B., Patterson, M. J., & Sifonis, C. M. (2004). The role of specificity and abstraction in creative idea generation. *Creativity Research Journal, 16*, 1–9.

Zabelina, D. L., & Robinson, M. D. (2010). Creativity as flexible cognitive control. *Psychology of Aesthetics, Creativity, and the Arts, 4*(3), 136.

MATHIEU CASSOTTI *is assistant professor of developmental psychology in the Laboratory for the Psychology of Child Development and Education (CNRS Unit 8240), Paris Descartes University, Sorbonne Paris Cité and Caen University, and junior member of the Institut Universitaire de France, France.*

MARINE AGOGUÉ *is assistant professor in the Department of Management, HEC Montréal, Canada.*

ANAËLLE CAMARDA *is a doctoral student in the Laboratory for the Psychology of Child Development and Education (CNRS Unit 8240), Paris Descartes University, Sorbonne Paris Cité and Caen University, France.*

OLIVIER HOUDÉ *is professor of developmental psychology in the Laboratory for the Psychology of Child Development and Education (CNRS Unit 8240), Paris Descartes University, Sorbonne Paris Cité and Caen University, and senior member of the Institut Universitaire de France, France.*

GRÉGOIRE BORST *is professor of developmental psychology in the Laboratory for the Psychology of Child Development and Education (CNRS Unit 8240), Paris Descartes University, Sorbonne Paris Cité and Caen University, France.*

New Directions for Child and Adolescent Development • DOI: 10.1002/cad

Kleibeuker, S. W., De Dreu, C. K. W., & Crone, E. A. (2016). Creativity development in adolescence: Insight from behavior, brain, and training studies. In B. Barbot (Ed.), *Perspectives
on creativity development. New Directions for Child and Adolescent Development, 151*, 73–84.

6

Creativity Development in Adolescence: Insight from Behavior, Brain, and Training Studies

Sietske W. Kleibeuker, Carsten K. W. De Dreu, Eveline A. Crone

Abstract

*Creativity is a multifaceted construct that recruits different cognitive processes.
Here, we summarize studies that show that creativity develops considerably
during adolescence with different developmental trajectories for insight, verbal
divergent thinking, and visuospatial divergent thinking. Next, these developmental time courses are mapped to changes in brain activity when individuals
perform divergent thinking tasks. The findings point to an important role of the
prefrontal cortex for generating novelty and complexity. Finally, the potentials
and limitations of training creativity in adolescence are described. The findings
are interpreted vis-à-vis the dynamic changes that occur during adolescence in
brain development and behavioral control processes. © 2016 Wiley Periodicals,
Inc.*

*C*reative thinking has been indicated as "the premier 21st century skill," and not without reason. In our current knowledge society, continuous innovation is critical, and information bases rapidly change and grow. Consequently, flexibility and the ability to think out of the box, to think divergently, and to generate and test multiple solutions to problems are valued more than ever before. Yet, whereas the importance of creative thinking in our society is undisputed, important gaps in our understanding of creativity remain. One key area that needs further investigation is the development of creative skills and competence. Does the ability to think creatively develop across childhood and adolescence, and how? Which neural mechanisms are involved during creative performance and, how (if possible) can creativity be improved?

From studies in related research fields, there is evidence that adolescence is a crucial period for the development of cognitive abilities (Casey, Jones, & Hare, 2008; Steinberg, 2005), and indeed, adolescents' brains demonstrate marked changes in structure and function (Luna, Padmanabhan, & O'Hearn, 2010; Shaw et al., 2008). Here we review recent studies on the development of creative thinking across adolescence to adulthood. We examine (a) the developmental trajectories of various aspects of creative thinking, (b) the development of underlying neural processes, and (c) the potential to improve creative thinking in adolescence through training.

The Development of Creative Thinking

Creativity is commonly referred to as the ability to generate ideas, insights, and solutions that are both original and feasible (e.g. Amabile, 1996; Sternberg & Lubart, 1996). As such, creative outcomes should be new and uncommon, yet also potentially useful and relevant; original but infeasible ideas are typically considered strange, whereas ideas that are feasible but not original are seen as mundane and, often, uninteresting. To understand the development of creative performance, this article builds upon the creative cognition approach, which identifies creative thinking as inherent to normal human cognitive functioning (Ward, Smith, & Finke, 1999) and emphasizes the dependence on fundamental cognitive functions, such as working memory and executive control (Nijstad, De Dreu, Rietzschel, & Baas, 2010).

Although the exact processes supporting creative outcomes are still under debate, there is growing consensus among scientists from social and cognitive (neuro)psychology that creative performance can be understood in terms of fast, implicit, and associative processing, and deliberate, effortful, and logical processing (Chaiken & Trope, 1999). This general notion has been further developed in the Dual Pathway to Creativity Model (De Dreu, Baas, & Nijstad, 2008), which describes creative outputs as the result of cognitive flexibility and cognitive persistence. Cognitive flexibility enables accessibility to multiple and broad cognitive categories, flexible switching between these categories, and a global processing style or broad focus (Förster, Friedman, & Lieberman, 2004). Cognitive persistence, in contrast, is associated with focused and systematic effort, in-depth exploration of a relatively small number of cognitive categories, and a local processing style or narrow focus (De Dreu et al., 2008). Indeed, a vast body of research has shown that creative performance can be achieved through both a flexible and divergent way of thinking as well as a persistent and systematic way of thinking (for a review, see Dietrich & Kanso, 2010). It is commonly assumed, as with other dual-process models, that creative outcomes are the product of both processing types, with different contribution ratios depending on the type of task to complete and individual functioning.

In a comprehensive behavioral study (Kleibeuker, De Dreu, & Crone, 2013a), we examined the development of two types of cognitive functions that represent creative potential: *divergent thinking* and *insight*. Divergent thinking is the most commonly tested function in creativity research and is considered an important component of the creative process, as it captures one's capacity to create novelty (Torrance, 1966). Divergent thinking tasks require the generation of multiple solutions to an open-ended problem (Guilford, 1967) and, being reflective of the cognitive flexibility pathway (Nijstad et al., 2010), divergent thinking has strong predictive value for creative success (Kim, 2008). Divergent thinking can be measured in different domains. We studied the Alternate Uses Task (AUT), which measures divergent thinking in the verbal domain, and the Creativity Ability Test (CAT), which measures divergent thinking in the visuospatial domain. The AUT explores a common task, which requires individuals to think of many unusual uses for a common object, for example, for a *brick*. The CAT involves predescribed rules that participants must adhere to when instructed to find as many matching figures as possible.

Participants in this study were in the age range 10–30 and creative performance on the divergent thinking tasks was expressed in terms of *fluency* (number of solutions), *flexibility* (generation of different conceptual categories), and *originality* (uniqueness or infrequency of solutions and ideas) (Guilford, 1967; Torrance, 1966). Thus, in terms of the Dual Pathway to Creativity Model (De Dreu et al., 2008), flexibility refers to a cognitive process including the ability to break, set, and use flat associative hierarchies of concepts, whereas fluency can be seen as an indicator of persistence (De Dreu et al., 2008).

The result of the developmental comparison study showed that on this version of the AUT, the capacity to generate multiple ideas (fluency) from different conceptual categories (flexibility) is already developed in adolescence but that the quality of solutions continues to develop (Figure 6.1). Possibly, with development adolescents gain knowledge from which associations can be made, and/or their better performance may reflect the development of cognitive processes that support the ability to flexibly coordinate between associative and analytic processing (Christoff, Gordon, & Smith,

Figure 6.1. Developmental Trajectories from Early Adolescence (Ages 12–13 Years) to Adulthood (Ages 25–30 Years) for (a) Insight, (b) Verbal Divergent Thinking and (c) Visuospatial Divergent Thinking

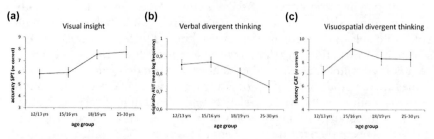

Source: Kleibeuker, S. W., De Dreu, C. K. W., & Crone, E. A. (2013a). The development of creative cognition across adolescence: Distinct trajectories for insight and divergent thinking. *Developmental Science,* 16(1), 2–12.
Note: (a) Mean ± 1 standard error (SEM) of the number of correct solutions for Snowy Picture Task. (b) Mean ± 1 standard error (SEM) of originality scores, represented by the mean frequency of solutions for Alternative Uses Task. Higher scores indicate less original solutions. (c) Mean ± 1 standard error (SEM) of the number of correct solutions for the Creative Ability Test. Reprinted with permission.

2009; Nijstad et al., 2010), an ability that develops only in late adolescence (Huizinga, Dolan, & van der Molen, 2006).

Some indirect support for the first explanation comes from the results for creative performance in the visuospatial CAT. Here we observed a relative advantage for middle adolescents for visuospatial divergent thinking compared to younger adolescent and young adults. Success is relatively independent of knowledge but requires generating and shifting between representations of the provided visual information, applying a set of rules, and monitoring behavior—cognitive functions that are commonly associated with prefrontal cortex (PFC) functioning and are still developing in adolescence (Huizinga et al., 2006). Possibly, middle adolescents have an advantage for explorative thinking (Johnson & Wilbrecht, 2011).

In addition to these divergent thinking tasks, participants completed insight tasks that, in contrast to divergent thinking tasks, have an established correct solution. This type of task generally requires establishing associations among unrelated or remotely related information and mentally restructuring the problem space (Förster et al., 2004). Insight solutions differ from noninsight solutions in that (a) solvers experience their solutions as sudden and have an "aha!" experience; (b) prior to producing an insight, solvers sometimes come to an impasse, a state of high uncertainty as to how to proceed; and (c) solvers usually cannot report the processing that led them to the solution. The tasks used in our study were the Gestalt Completion Task (GCT; Eckstrom, French, Harman, & Dermen, 1976), the Snowy Picture Task (SPT; Eckstrom et al., 1976), and the Remote Associates Task

NEW DIRECTIONS FOR CHILD AND ADOLESCENT DEVELOPMENT • DOI: 10.1002/cad

(RAT; Mednick, 1962). The first two tasks (GCT and SPT) capture insight ability in the visual domain whereas the RAT focuses on insight ability in the verbal domain. We observed that creative insight (both visual and verbal) continued to develop into late adolescence. Noteworthy are the differential patterns of the developmental trajectories, which were best described by step-wise (visual) and curvilinear (verbal) models. In particular, results in the visual domain were indicative of qualitative changes in underlying cognitive processes (see also Uhlhaas et al., 2009).

In summary, these results supported the distinctiveness of creativity aspects and indicate both immaturities (insight, verbal divergent thinking originality) and creative potentials (visuospatial divergent thinking) during different stages of adolescence. These findings of different developmental time courses fit with prior studies indicating that creativity performances improve with age from childhood throughout adolescence (e.g., Lau & Cheung, 2010, Runco & Bahleda, 1986), but that performance slumps may occur at different stages in adolescence (Lau & Cheung, 2010; see also Wu, Cheng, Ip, & McBride-Chang, 2005 for a comparison between adolescents and adults).

Neural Correlates of Creativity

Neuroimaging is a useful method for gaining insight into the processes underlying creative success. In recent years, several researchers have investigated creative cognition using lesion studies and neuroimaging techniques, including functional magnetic resonance imaging (fMRI). Results are, however, not yet conclusive about the neural underpinnings of this complex construct (Arden, Chavez, Grazioplene, & Jung, 2010; Dietrich & Kanso, 2010), and differences between study outcomes are likely related to the various measures capturing different aspects of creative thinking. Despite this, there is consensus that the lateral parts of PFC play a role in creative success. This brain region is generally associated with cognitive control functioning and coordinating lower level (associative) brain regions (e.g., Miller & Cohen, 2001) and is involved in both insight and divergent thinking tasks (see, for example, Arden et al., 2010; Dietrich & Kanso, 2010). Interestingly, this brain region still shows substantial changes over the course of adolescence (Mills & Tamnes, 2014). We therefore examined possible differences in neural activation between adolescence and adults when performing verbal and visuospatial insight tasks.

To tap into the underpinnings of creative cognition in the verbal divergent thinking domain, we adapted the AUT for use in an experimental imaging design. A relatively consistent finding across studies that have used the AUT in adults is the involvement of (left) temporoparietal regions, including the angular gyrus (AG) and the supramarginal gyrus (SMG) (Arden et al., 2010; Dietrich & Kanso, 2010). Notably, a substantial part of these studies revealed positive relations between PFC activations and creative performance (e.g., Carlsson, Wendt, & Risberg, 2000; Chavez-Eakle, Graf-Guerrero, Garcia-Reyna, Vaugier, & Cruz-Fuentes, 2007; Gibson, Folley, & Park, 2009). We investigated the neurodevelopmental changes of verbal creative idea generation in adolescents and adults (Kleibeuker et al., 2013c). Based on the behavioral study described earlier, we predicted that adults (25–30 years) would outperform adolescents (15–17 years) on creative idea generation, and indeed, adults generated significantly more alternative uses than adolescents. Furthermore, the fMRI results indicated involvement of a temporoparietal network including the left angular gyrus (AG), the left supramarginal gyrus (SMG), and the bilateral middle temporal gyrus (MTG) in both adults and adolescents (Figure 6.2). Interestingly, trials with only *multiple* solutions, a hallmark of divergent thinking, resulted in additional left inferior frontal gyrus (IFG)/middle frontal gyrus (MFG) activation. Possibly, the ability to generate multiple ideas (viz. divergent thinking), involves cognitive control functioning, such as attentional inhibition and cognitive flexibility (see, for example, De Dreu et al., 2012). Notably, activations in these frontal regions were more pronounced in adults than adolescents.

To examine the processes underlying visuospatial creative problem solving we made use of the matchstick problem tasks (MPT; Guilford,

Figure 6.2. (a) Brain Regions Involved in Verbal Divergent Thinking Based on the Alternative Uses Task and (b) Brain Regions Involved in Visuospatial Divergent Thinking Based on the Matchstick Task

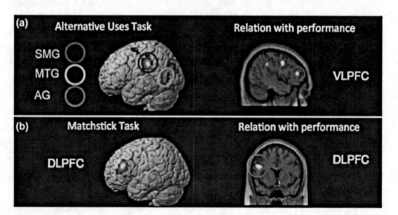

Sources: Kleibeuker, S. W., Koolschijn, P. C. M. P., Jolles, D. D., De Dreu, C. K. W., & Crone, E. A. (2013b). The neural coding of creative idea generation across adolescence and early adulthood. *Frontiers in Human Neuroscience, 7,* 905; Kleibeuker, S. W., Koolschijn, P. C. M. P., Jolles, D. D., Schel, M. A., De Dreu, C. K. W., & Crone, E. A. (2013c). Prefrontal cortex involvement in creative problem solving in middle adolescence and adulthood. *Developmental Cognitive Neuroscience, 5,* 197–206.
Note: SMG = supramarginal gyrus, MTG = middle temporal gyrus, AG = angular gyrus, DLPFC = dorsolateral prefrontal cortex, VLPFC = ventrolateral prefrontal cortex. Reprinted with permission.

1967), which presents the participants with classic divergent thinking problems. An MPT involves an arrangement of matches that must be reorganized to make other predescribed patterns by removing a number of matchsticks. To solve this kind of problem, one is required to overcome mental fixation of the initially presented formation of matchsticks (Guilford, 1967). Prior neuropsychological and brain imaging studies using MPT and related tasks revealed the involvement of the lateral PFC in creative problem solving (Goel & Vartanian, 2005).

In our study, adolescents (15–17 years) and adults (25–30 years) were subjected to both an MPT, while scanning neural activation with fMRI, and the previously used visuospatial divergent thinking task (creative ability task; CAT) outside the scanner (Kleibeuker, Koolschijn, Jolles, De Dreu, & Crone, 2013b). Interestingly, adolescents outperformed adults on experimental problems (seeking alternative solutions for the MPT), indicating an advantage for this age group for problems that require exploration and shifting between representations. Solving the MPT problems was associated with increased activity in IFG and dorsolateral PFC (DLPFC) (Figure 6.2). A direct comparison between age groups revealed increased activation in left (IFG) and right (DLPFC) during successful creative problem solving for adolescents compared to adults. Individual difference analyses demonstrated a positive relation between creative problem-solving performance and activity in left IFG. Prior research suggests particular relevance of left IFG for switching between representations (Crone, Wendelken, Donohue, van Leijenhorst, & Bunge, 2006; Hirshorn & Thompson-Schill, 2006). Moreover, activation in right DLPFC was associated with better visuospatial divergent thinking capacities (CAT performance). Thus, individuals with greater visuospatial thinking abilities recruited right DLPFC during creative problem solving more than individuals with poor visuospatial thinking abilities. This study, therefore, supports the hypothesis that adolescence is not only a phase of immaturity but also a period of enhanced PFC activation for exploration and adaptive purposes (Crone & Dahl, 2012).

Creative Ideation Training in Adolescence

Various studies have already demonstrated the effectiveness of training paradigms in improving creativity in both adults (Kienitz et al., 2014) and children (Cliatt, Shaw, & Sherwood, 1980). However, relatively little is known about how malleable creative thinking is in adolescence. Training studies in other higher cognitive skills include working memory (Jolles & Crone, 2012; Klingberg, 2010), executive control (Karbach & Kray, 2009; Zinke, Einert, Pfennig, & Kliegel, 2012), and algebraic equation solving (Qin et al., 2004), and emphasize the training susceptibility regarding performance and brain function during adolescence.

NEW DIRECTIONS FOR CHILD AND ADOLESCENT DEVELOPMENT • DOI: 10.1002/cad

In a behavioral training study (Stevenson, Kleibeuker, De Dreu, & Crone, 2014), we applied a simple creative ideation training paradigm. The main aim of the study was to examine whether creative ideation could be improved by practicing alternative uses generation in adolescents (13–16 years) and adults (23–30 years). In this study, participants followed one of three training types, each composed of eight 20-minute practice sessions within 2 weeks: (a) alternative uses generation (creative ideation, experimental condition), (b) object characteristic naming (general ideation, control condition), or (c) global local rule switching (rule switching, control condition). Performance prior to training sessions resembled previous research and revealed that adolescents already performed at adult level on ideational fluency and flexibility and that adults outperformed adolescents on originality measures. Posttraining results demonstrated that participants in general (irrespective of age group and training condition) progressed on creative ideation originality and fluency. With regard to originality, adolescents progressed further after 2 weeks of training than adults, independent of the type of training. Possibly, this indicates greater practice susceptibility for adolescents than for adults, consistent with the hypothesis that adolescence is a period of enhanced flexibility in cognition and learning (Crone & Dahl, 2012; Johnson & Wilbrecht, 2011).

Important new questions triggered by these results are what (brain) mechanisms are underlying training success in adolescents and to what extent training effects are related to the reorganization of the PFC and associated regulatory systems during adolescence (Keating, 2004; Steinberg, 2005). To examine these issues, we asked participants aged 15–16 years to perform an adapted version of the AUT (similar to the task described in Kleibeuker et al., 2013c); fMRI images were acquired before and after the training program (Kleibeuker et al., 2015). Again, the core brain regions for creative ideation (SMG, AG, MTG) were consistently activated in adolescents and recruitment remained relatively stable after training. The results further demonstrated involvement of lateral PFC in creative ideation output, establishing that performance change, irrespective of training, was positively associated with activation change in IFG/MFG. This further indicates that lateral PFC activation is predictive of divergent thinking success. The exact functions of lateral PFC regions in divergent thinking still need to be deciphered. Future research should therefore distinguish between different aspects of the creative process and examine the relation between lateral PFC regions and the brain networks that support these divergent thinking aspects.

Conclusion

This review highlights the distinctiveness of developmental trajectories for the different cognitive processes underlying creative performance, with a relative peak for middle adolescents' visuospatial divergent thinking

NEW DIRECTIONS FOR CHILD AND ADOLESCENT DEVELOPMENT • DOI: 10.1002/cad

whereas adults outperformed adolescents on verbal idea generation. Interestingly, success for both types of creative tasks was related to lateral PFC activations so that, relative to adults, middle adolescents showed increased activity for visuospatial divergent thinking and decreased activity for verbal divergent thinking in these late developing brain regions.

It is important to recognize the complexity of creativity, which recruits distinct cognitive processes and takes on different meaning in different task domains. Although we captured creative performance in terms of its hallmarks—originality and insight—we also focused on a limited set of cognitive processes—divergent thinking in particular. Accordingly, and notwithstanding the fact that divergent thinking has been widely recognized as essential and predictive for creativity success (e.g., Kim, 2008; Nijstad et al., 2010), some reservations should be made regarding the generalizability of the results. For example, the Dual Pathway to Creativity Model (De Dreu et al., 2008) would predict that in addition to divergent thinking and cognitive flexibility, creativity can be achieved also through effortful and persistent processing. The work reviewed here did not focus on such effortful processing as a possible means toward creativity, and future studies are needed to uncover whether and how adolescents may differ from adults in this otherwise vital process. In addition, we used simple practice paradigms to gain insight into the trainability of creative thinking in adolescence. An interesting direction for future research is also to test in more detail the relation with executive functions such as working memory, inhibition, and relational reasoning. Nonetheless, the current findings provide important insights into the functionality of the adolescent brain when confronted with problems that require out-of-the-box thinking. Accordingly, the findings summarized here can serve as a useful starting point to model the relationship between neurocognitive development that recognizes the complexity of functional brain development during the transitional phase of adolescence and the vital cognitive processes underlying creativity in both verbal and visuospatial domains of performance. Such modeling could provide useful implications for educational purposes as a better understanding of how the adolescent brain processes information and generates opportunities to adjust educational programs to optimize successful processing of learning material.

References

Amabile, T. M. (1996). *Creativity in context: Update to "The social psychology of creativity."* Boulder, CO: Westview Press.

Arden, R., Chavez, R. S., Grazioplene, R., & Jung, R. E. (2010). Neuroimaging creativity: A psychometric view. *Behavioural Brain Research, 214*(2), 143–156.

Carlsson. I., Wendt, P. E., & Risberg, J. (2000). On the neurobiology of creativity. Differences in frontal activity between high and low creative subjects. *Neuropsychologia, 38,* 873–885.

Casey, B. J., Jones, R. M., & Hare, T. A. (2008). The adolescent brain. *Annals of the New York Academy of Sciences, 1124*, 111–126.

Chaiken, S., & Trope, Y. (Eds.). (1999). *Dual-process theories in social psychology.* Guilford Press.

Chavez-Eakle, R., Graf-Guerrero, A., Garcia-Reyna, J., Vaugier, V., & Cruz-Fuentes, C. (2007). Cerebral blood flow associated with creative performance: A comparative study. *NeuroImage, 38,* 519–528.

Christoff, K., Gordon, A., & Smith, R. (2009). The role of spontaneous thought in human cognition. In O. Vartanian & D. R. Mandel (Eds.), *Neuroscience of decision making.* New York: Psychology Press.

Cliatt, M. J. P., Shaw, J. M., & Sherwood, J. M. (1980). Effects of training on the divergent thinking abilities of kindergarten children. *Child Development, 51*(4), 1061–1064.

Crone, E. A., & Dahl, R. E. (2012). Understanding adolescence as a period of social-affective engagement and goal flexibility. *Nature Reviews. Neuroscience, 13*(9), 636–650.

Crone, E. A., Wendelken, C., Donohue, S., van Leijenhorst, L., & Bunge, S. A. (2006). Neurocognitive development of the ability to manipulate information in working memory. *Proceedings of the National Academy of Sciences, 103*(24), 9315–9320.

De Dreu, C. K. W., Baas, M., & Nijstad, B. A. (2008). Hedonic tone and activation level in the mood-creativity link: Toward a dual pathway to creativity model. *Journal of Personality and Social Psychology, 94*(5), 739–756.

De Dreu, C. K., Nijstad, B. A., Baas, M., Wolsink, I., & Roskes, M. (2012). Working memory benefits creative insight, musical improvisation, and original ideation through maintained task-focused attention. *Personality and Social Psychology Bulletin, 38*(5), 656–669.

Dietrich, A., & Kanso, R. (2010). A review of EEG, ERP, and neuroimaging studies of creativity and insight. *Psychological Bulletin, 136*(5), 822–848.

Eckstrom, R. B., French, J. W., Harman, M. H., & Dermen, D. (1976). *Manual for kit of factor-referenced cognitive tests.* Princeton, NJ: Educational Testing Service.

Förster, J., Friedman, R. S., & Liberman, N. (2004). Temporal construal effects on abstract and concrete thinking: Consequences for insight and creative cognition. *Journal of Personality and Social Psychology, 87*(2), 177–189.

Gibson, C., Folley, B. S., & Park, S. (2009). Enhanced divergent thinking and creativity in musicians: A behavioral and near-infrared spectroscopy study. *Brain and Cognition, 69*, 162–169.

Goel, V., & Vartanian, O. (2005). Dissociating the roles of right ventral lateral and dorsal lateral prefrontal cortex in generation and maintenance of hypotheses in set-shift problems. *Cerebral Cortex, 15*(8), 1170–1177.

Guilford, J. P. (1967). *The nature of human intelligence.* New York: McGraw-Hill.

Hirshorn, E. A., & Thompson-Schill, S. H., (2006). Role of the left inferior frontal gyrus in covert word retrieval: Neural correlates of switching during verbal fluency. *Neuropsychologia, 44*(12), 2547–2557.

Huizinga, M., Dolan, C. V., & van der Molen, M. W. (2006). Age-related change in executive function: Developmental trends and a latent variable analysis. *Neuropsychologia, 44*(11), 2017–2036.

Johnson, C., & Wilbrecht, L. (2011). Juvenile mice show greater flexibility in multiple choice reversal learning than adults. *Developmental Cognitive Neuroscience, 1*(4), 540–551.

Jolles, D. D., & Crone, E. A. (2012). Training the developing brain: A neurocognitive perspective. *Frontiers in Human Neuroscience, 6*, 76.

Karbach, J., & Kray, J. (2009). How useful is executive control training? Age differences in near and far transfer of task-switching training. *Developmental Science, 12*(6), 978–990.

Keating, D. P. (2004). Cognitive and brain development. In R. M. Lerner & L. Steinberg (Eds.), *Handbook of adolescent psychology* (2nd ed., pp. 45–84). New York: John Wiley & Sons.

Kienitz, E., Quintin, E.-M., Saggar, M., Bott, N. T., Royalty, A., Hong, D. W-C., et al. (2014). Targeted intervention to increase creative capacity and performance: A randomized controlled pilot study. *Thinking Skills and Creativity, 13*, 57–66.

Kim, K. H. (2008). Meta-analyses of the relationship of creative achievement to both IQ and divergent thinking test scores. *Journal of Creative Behavior, 42*(2), 106–130.

Kleibeuker, S. W., De Dreu, C. K. W., & Crone, E. A. (2013a). The development of creative cognition across adolescence: Distinct trajectories for insight and divergent thinking. *Developmental Science, 16*(1), 2–12.

Kleibeuker, S. W., Koolschijn, P. C. M. P., Jolles, D. D., De Dreu, C. K. W., & Crone, E. A. (2013b). The neural coding of creative idea generation across adolescence and early adulthood. *Frontiers in Human Neuroscience, 7*, 905. doi: 10.3389/fnhum.2013.00905

Kleibeuker, S. W., Koolschijn, P. C. M. P., Jolles, D. D., Schel, M. A., De Dreu, C. K. W., & Crone, E. A. (2013c). Prefrontal cortex involvement in creative problem solving in middle adolescence and adulthood. *Developmental Cognitive Neuroscience, 5*, 197–206.

Kleibeuker, S. W., Stevenson, C. E., Van der Aar, L., Overgaauw, S., Van Duijvenvoorde, A. C., Crone, E. A. (2015). Training in the adolescent brain: An fMRI training study on divergent thinking. Manuscipt in preparation.

Klingberg, T. (2010). Training and plasticity of working memory. *Trends in Cognitive Sciences, 14*(7), 317–324.

Lau, S., & Cheung, P. C. (2010). Developmental trends of creativity: What twists of turn do boys and girls take at different grades? *Creativity Research Journal, 22*(3), 329–336.

Luna, B., Padmanabhan, A., & O'Hearn, K. (2010). What has fMRI told us about the development of cognitive control through adolescence? *Brain and Cognition, 72*(1), 101–113.

Miller, E. K., & Cohen, J. D. (2001). An integrative theory of prefrontal cortex function. *Annual Review of Neuroscience, 24*(1), 167–202.

Mills, K. L., & Tamnes, C. K. (2014). Methods and considerations for longitudinal structural brain imaging analysis across development. *Developmental Cognitive Neuroscience, 9*, 172–190.

Mednick, S. A. (1962). The associative basis of the creative process. *Psychological Review, 69*, 220–232.

Nijstad, B. A., De Dreu, C. K. W., Rietzschel, E. F., & Baas, M. (2010). The dual pathway to creativity model: Creative ideation as a function of flexibility and persistence. *European Review of Social Psychology, 21*, 34–77.

Qin, Y., Carter, C. S., Silk, E. M., Stenger, V. A., Fissell, K., Goode, A., et al. (2004). The change of the brain activation patterns as children learn algebra equation solving. *Proceedings of the National Academy of Sciences, 101*(15), 5686–5691.

Runco, M. A., & Bahleda, M. D. (1986). Implicit theories of artistic, scientific, and everyday creativity. *Journal of Creative Behavior, 20*(2), 93–98

Shaw, P., Kabani, N. J., Lerch, J. P., Eckstrand, K., Lenroot, R., Gogtay, N., et al. (2008). Neurodevelopmental trajectories of the human cerebral cortex. *Journal of Neuroscience, 28*, 3586–3594.

Steinberg, L. (2005). Cognitive and affective development in adolescence. *Trends in Cognitive Sciences, 9*(2), 69–74.

Sternberg, R. J., & Lubart, T. (1996). Investing in creativity. *American Psychologist, 51*(7), 677–688.

Stevenson, C. E., Kleibeuker, S. W., De Dreu, C. K. W., & Crone, E. A. (2014). Training creative cognition: Adolescence as a flexible period for improving creativity. *Frontiers in Human Neuroscience, 8*, 827. doi: 10.3389/fnhum.2014.00827

Torrance, E. P. (1966). *Torrance tests of creative thinking*. Princeton, NJ: Personnel Press.

Uhlhaas, P. J., Roux, F., Singer, W., Haenschel, C., Sireteanu, R., & Rodriguez, E. (2009). The development of neural synchrony reflects late maturation and restructuring of functional networks in humans. *Proceedings of the National Academy of Sciences*, *106*(24), 9866–9871.

Ward, T. B., Smith, S. M., & Finke, R. A. (1999). Creative cognition. In R. J. Sternberg (Ed.), *Handbook of creativity* (pp. 189–212). New York: Cambridge University Press.

Wu, C. H., Cheng, Y., Ip, H. M., & McBride-Chang, C. (2005). Age differences in creativity: Task structure and knowledge base. *Creativity Research Journal*, *17*, 321–326.

Zinke, K., Einert, M., Pfennig, L., & Kliegel, M. (2012). Plasticity of executive control through task switching training in adolescents. *Frontiers in Human Neuroscience*, *6*, 41. doi: 10.3389/fnhum.2012.00041

SIETSKE W. KLEIBEUKER is PhD student at the Institute of Psychology, Leiden University, the Netherlands.

CARSTEN K. W. DE DREU is professor of psychology and behavioral economics at the University of Amsterdam Department of Psychology and Center for Experimental Economics and Political Decision Making.

EVELINE A. CRONE is professor of neurocognitive developmental psychology at the Institute of Psychology, Leiden University, the Netherlands.

Beghetto, R. A. & Dilley, A. E. (2016). Creative aspirations or pipe dreams? Toward understanding creative mortification in children and adolescents. In B. Barbot (Ed.), *Perspectives on creativity development. New Directions for Child and Adolescent Development, 151*, 85–95.

7

Creative Aspirations or Pipe Dreams? Toward Understanding Creative Mortification in Children and Adolescents

Ronald A. Beghetto, Anna E. Dilley

Abstract

What experiences influence the development of creativity in children and adolescents? One experience is the mortification of creative aspirations. Creative mortification (CM) refers to the loss of one's willingness to pursue a particular creative aspiration following a negative performance outcome. The purpose of this article is to introduce an empirically testable model of CM. Specifically, the model highlights how CM can result from interpreting a negative performance outcome through the lens of internal attributions, fixed ability beliefs, and the experience of shame. The model further posits that young people's level of aspirational commitment, the feedback they receive, and their sociocultural context can moderate their interpretations and experiences of negative performance outcomes and CM. © 2016 Wiley Periodicals, Inc.

C hildhood and adolescence represent key developmental periods in which young people explore and engage in various forms of creative expression (e.g., dance, writing, science, drawing, sports). These early experiences play a critical role in developing creative aspirations into creative identities. We define creative identity as a self-perception that a particular creative activity has been incorporated into one's sense of self (e.g., "I am a dancer," "I am a poet"). One way to think about the development of creative identity is along a trajectory (Beghetto, 2013) starting with an exploratory interest ("I like writing poems"), developing into an aspirational commitment ("I'm going to be a poet when I grow up"), and ultimately becoming part of one's personal identity ("I'm a poet").

As young people develop their creative identity, they are also developing their competence related to that creative activity. Competence development takes many years of intense, deliberate practice (Ericsson, 1996). Along the way, young people will experience various setbacks. These setbacks can range from being told they are performing a rehearsed skill incorrectly, making mistakes during a performance, or being told by a teacher or coach that they are not ready to advance to the next level. Such setbacks occur in various contexts (e.g., group practice sessions; public performance; one-on-one interactions with teachers, parents, and coaches) and serve as opportunities to identify strengths and build on weaknesses. In this way, developing competence involves learning from both successes and failures.

Accomplished creators have learned how to receive and act on negative performance-related outcomes and feedback (Bandura, 1997; Beghetto, 2013; Cianci, Klein, & Seijts, 2010). Moreover, a celebrated trait of many accomplished creators is that they have "defied the crowd" (Sternberg & Lubart, 1995) in pursuit of their creative aspirations. This involves being able to persist in one's creative pursuits in the face of setbacks. Although working through setbacks is necessary for developing competence and ultimately one's creative identity, not all young people experience setbacks in the same way.

Two children of similar ability levels may, for instance, experience a dance instructor's negative critique in opposite ways. One may feel angered by the feedback and endeavor to practice twice as hard so as to prove the instructor wrong. The other may be so devastated by the comments that she loses the desire to dance ballet ever again. The latter experience refers to what has been called "creative mortification" (Beghetto, 2013, 2014). Creative mortification (CM) is the loss of one's willingness to pursue a particular creative aspiration following a negative performance outcome (Beghetto, 2014). The experience of CM can stifle the development of one's creative identity and result in *talent loss* (Hong & Milgram, 2008). Talent loss, in this context, refers to the failure of realizing one's creative potential and can exact an immeasurable toll on aspiring creators.

Although it is possible for CM to occur anytime across the life span, young people—particularly those in the throes of adolescence—may be

NEW DIRECTIONS FOR CHILD AND ADOLESCENT DEVELOPMENT • DOI: 10.1002/cad

more vulnerable to CM. Indeed, previous scholars have asserted that the transition from childhood to adolescence tends to be a critical time with respect to the abandonment of creative aspirations (see Albert, 1996, for a review). One reason this might be the case is that this period is marked by the development of one's identity and the experience of multiple sources of feedback on one's aspirations. A key question for researchers and practitioners interested in supporting young people's creative competence is: *What factors lead to the mortification of their creative aspirations?* The purpose of this short article is to explore this question by way of introducing an empirically testable model and applying that model to two brief examples.

Process Model of Creative Mortification

Creative mortification can be thought of as resulting from a confluence of factors. The process model[1] displayed in Figure 7.1 elaborates on previous theoretical and empirical work (Beghetto, 2013, 2014) and highlights how several key factors can work together to result in CM.

As illustrated in Figure 7.1, we assert that CM can result from interpreting a negative performance outcome through the lens of internal attributions, fixed ability beliefs, and the experience of shame. We further assert that young people's level of aspirational commitment, the feedback they receive, and the sociocultural context can moderate their interpretations and experiences of negative performance outcomes and CM. In the following sections, we elaborate on these assertions.

Negative Performance Outcomes.

Assertion 1: Negative performance outcomes set the stage for creative mortification. The development of creative competence and, in turn, one's

Figure 7.1. Process Model of Creative Mortification

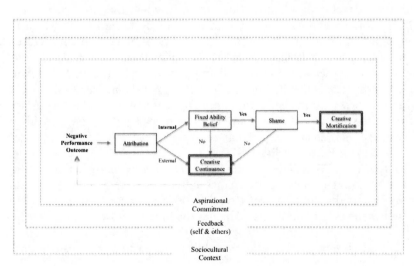

creative identity involves receiving and acting on performance-related feedback. Given that aspiring creators are still developing their competence, they are more likely to make mistakes compared to more competent creators. As a result, they are also more likely to receive negative, and potentially harsh, feedback (Bandura, 1997). The negative "feedback" on the deficient performance can come from various sources. Those sources include the self (e.g., self-judging the performance as falling short of how one imagined it would be), others (e.g., receiving devaluing feedback from parents, teachers, and coaches), or some combination thereof. Regardless of the source, we assert that if young people ultimately interpret a performance outcome in a negative light, then they will be vulnerable to experiencing CM.

Internal Attributions.

Assertion 2: Creative mortification results from an internal attribution of failure. As illustrated in Figure 7.1, the causal attributions a young person makes following a negative performance outcome will influence whether he or she will continue to pursue creative aspirations or, instead, experience CM. Two types of attributions are relevant to this model: *global-self* and *external-other* (Lewis & Sullivan, 2005; Weiner, 1985). Global-self attributions refer to blaming oneself for a failure (e.g., "I'm a complete failure...I'll never be a dancer"). Conversely, external-other attributions refer to externalizing responsibility for the failure (e.g., "My dance instructor doesn't like me and refuses to see my potential"). It is also possible for a person to attribute failure to a combination of internal and external causes (e.g., "I lack the talent and supportive teachers necessary to be a dancer").

Of concern to CM is whether young people blame themselves for failure. When young people move beyond initial exploration of a domain ("I like dancing") and move toward personally identifying with that domain ("I am a dancer"), then their creative aspirations become entangled with their developing identity. Consequently, when they experience negative performance outcomes they are more likely to be in a self-focused state of attention, which increases the chances of blaming themselves for failure (see Tracy & Robins, 2006). This makes them vulnerable to viewing those outcomes as a "global indictment of the self" (Lewis & Sullivan, 2005) and increases the likelihood of experiencing shame (see Assertion 4). When coupled with the belief that improvement is not possible (see Assertion 3), they may feel like they have run into a dead end and be more likely to abandon their creative aspirations.

Holding a Fixed Ability Belief.

Assertion 3: Fixed ability beliefs can lead to creative mortification. Young people interpret negative performance outcomes through the lens of the ability beliefs they hold. Carol Dweck (2006) has described these beliefs as "self-theories" or "mindsets." She has distinguished two core ability beliefs: *fixed* (or entity) mindsets and *growth* (or incremental) mindsets. A fixed mindset refers to the belief that ability in a particular domain is static and cannot improve. A growth mindset refers to the belief that one's ability can increase with effort. People who hold fixed beliefs tend to avoid subsequent performance opportunities after experiencing failure. Conversely, those who hold growth beliefs are motivated to improve upon past failures.

With respect to the development of creative aspirations, if young people hold fixed ability beliefs, then they will be more likely to give up on their creative aspirations after experiencing negative performance outcomes. Prior empirical work has provided initial support for this assertion (Beghetto, 2014)[2] and this assertion also makes practical sense. Specifically, if young people hold a fixed mindset, then they likely would view the continued pursuit of a failed attempt as an exercise in futility. Consequently, they would be more likely to experience CM.

Experiencing Shame.

Assertion 4: Young people who experience shame likely will experience creative mortification. Young people will be more likely to experience CM if they experience shame as a result of a negative performance outcome. This assertion has its basis in existing programs of research that have described the stifling impact that experiencing shame can have on subsequent behavior (Lewis & Sullivan, 2005; Scheff, 2003; Tracy & Robins, 2006) and prior theoretical and empirical work that has linked shame to CM (Beghetto, 2013, 2014).

Shame is a powerful, negative self-conscious emotion. Self-conscious emotions differ from basic emotions (like anger, fear, sadness) because they result from attributing events and outcomes to internal causes (see Assertion 2; Lewis & Sullivan, 2005; Tracy & Robins, 2006). The experience of shame can trigger an intense and lasting avoidant response. As Lewis and Sullivan (2005) have explained, "all that someone can do when shamed is attempt somehow to be rid of it" (p. 190). If young people experience shame as the result of pursuing a creative aspiration, then they will be more vulnerable to abandoning that aspiration.

Creative Mortification.

Assertion 5: Creative mortification results from experiencing shame, holding fixed ability beliefs, and making internal attributions of failure following a negative performance outcome. Taken together, we assert that CM will result from a combination of subjective interpretations of a negative performance outcome (Assertion 1)—specifically, blaming oneself for failure (Assertion 2), holding fixed ability beliefs (Assertion 3), and experiencing shame (Assertion 4). We also recognize that the experience of CM can be moderated by various factors, including differing levels of commitment to a creative aspiration (Assertion 7), the feedback one receives after a negative performance outcome (Assertion 8), and one's sociocultural context (Assertion 9).

Creative Continuance.

Assertion 6: Young people will be more likely to continue pursuing their creative aspiration if they externalize failure, hold growth beliefs, and do not feel shamed by negative performance outcomes. There are various factors that can result in creative continuance. With respect to our process model, the key factors that we have specified include externalizing failure, holding growth beliefs, and not feeling shamed. Some of these factors (e.g., growth mindset) are more positive and sustainable than others (e.g., externalizing failure). If one's competence is low, for instance, a young person may ignore or externalize that failure. Indeed, there is evidence that incompetence may be a key factor in overestimating one's actual ability (Kruger & Dunning, 1999). It is possible, however, that externalizing failure can, at times, be adaptive. A young person may, for instance, view a critique as unjust, brush it away, and even use it as motivation (e.g., "I will prove that teacher wrong...I will be a poet!"). Still, externalizing critiques is not a sustainable long-term strategy. Rather, in order to develop creative aspirations into creative accomplishments, young people need to take ownership of their negative performance outcomes so they can build on their strengths and address their weaknesses (Bandura, 1997; Beghetto, 2013; Kaufman & Beghetto, 2013).

Aspirational Commitment.

Assertion 7: Variations in aspirational commitment will moderate creative mortification. We define aspirational commitment (AC) as the level of interest, personal investment, and competence a young person has in a particular creative pursuit. Our conceptualization is informed by prior theory and research on interest development (Hidi & Renniger, 2006; Krapp, 2002). Along these lines, we posit that differing levels of aspirational commitment will moderate the experience of CM. Specifically, we would predict that a young person with low or superficial aspirational commitment (e.g., "writing poetry is fun"), would be less likely to experience CM after a negative outcome because he or she is not personally invested in poetry and thereby may not internalize the failure or experience shame.

We would further predict that a young person with a deeply established commitment to his or her aspiration would also be buffered from mortification but for a different reason. Deeply established aspirational commitment entails fully identifying with the creative endeavor (e.g., "I am a poet") and being recognized by others as assuming that creative identity (e.g., "You are a poet"). By the time a young person has developed deep aspirational commitment he or she would likely have also developed competence in that domain. We assert that competence can promote resilience and thereby buffer the experience of CM. Indeed, people with greater domain expertise tend to gravitate toward and respond more favorably to negative feedback (see Finkelstein & Fishbach, 2011). It is, of course, possible for a young person to believe that he is a poet, and even have others tell him he is a poet, but have low levels of actual competence. In such a situation, we would classify that person as being more vulnerable to CM in the long run than someone who has developed actual competence. Real-world constraints eventually catch up with misperceived levels of competence.

Finally, we would predict that young people with more moderate levels of aspirational commitment would be most vulnerable to experiencing CM. One reason is because they have started identifying with the domain (e.g., "I want to be a poet") and thereby would be more likely to internalize a negative performance outcome but have not developed enough competence to buffer themselves from CM. They thereby might be more susceptible to domain-specific clichés that endorse fixed ability beliefs (e.g., "some people are born to be great poets") and more susceptible to the experience of shame following negative performance outcomes (e.g., "I guess I'm not the poet I thought I was ... ").

Feedback

Assertion 8: Feedback (from self or others) will moderate experiences of creative mortification. Feedback likely plays a critical role in how young people interpret and experience performance outcomes. Feedback can influence whether young people blame themselves (or external circumstances) for failure and setbacks in pursuit of their aspirations (Assertions 1 and 2). Feedback can also influence whether young people believe improvement is possible (Dweck, 2006, Assertion 3), the emotions they experience (Lewis & Sullivan, 2005; Tracy & Robins, 2006; Assertion 4), and ultimately their experience of CM (Assertion 5). We thereby assert that feedback (from oneself and others) can serve as either a buffer or a catalyst in the process of CM.

Sociocultural Context.

Assertion 9: Sociocultural context will moderate experiences of creative mortification. Context matters when it comes to how young people interpret negative performance outcomes. Indeed, motivational beliefs and emotional reactions are somewhat malleable and can be influenced by the particular sociocultural features of a performance environment. A growth versus fixed mindset, for instance, can be influenced by the kinds of feedback received before and after a performance (Dweck, 2006). Moreover, certain performance domains may have their own well-established norms for critiquing performance (e.g., "You have to have thick skin to be successful in this profession"). Familiarity and endorsement of those norms may temper the way young people experience negative performance outcomes. In short, the sociocultural context matters. Consequently, we predict that the particular temporal, spatial, and sociocultural features of a given context will play a nontrivial role in shaping how young people interpret and experience negative performance outcomes.

Applying the Model

At this point, it may be helpful to apply the model to the two brief examples.[3] One example highlights how a negative performance outcome can result in the mortification of creative aspirations and the other high-lights how it can result in the continuance of creative aspirations.

Creative Mortification Example. The following example is based on a vignette published in the *Rhode Island Schoolmaster* (DeMunn & Snow, 1865, p. 88). The vignette focuses on a child (Jane) who had aspirations to become a singer. One day as Jane was singing with her classmates, her teacher stopped her and asked, "Jane, what are you trying to sing? The tune sung by the old cow when she died? What a discord!" Jane stopped singing in this moment "dropped her head upon the desk, and the bitter tears ran down her cheeks" (DeMunn & Snow, 1865, p. 88). Her classmates laughed at the teacher's remark and then continued to sing without Jane. Seeing how Jane reacted, the teacher was sorry for the remark and thought Jane would soon forget about it. Jane did not forget, "the remembrance of those words would always remain with Jane, to keep her, in future, from the vain attempt to sing" (DeMunn & Snow, 1865, p. 88). Even though Jane "cherished the idea of becoming a singer" she would no longer pursue her aspiration and, instead, chose to "bury the desire, rather than subject herself to ridicule again." (DeMunn & Snow, 1865, p. 88).

Working backwards from our model, we can see how this is an example of CM. Specifically, Jane, an aspiring singer, "buried the desire" to become a singer after one particular negative performance outcome. More-over, that moment "remained with her" and kept her from pursuing the "vain attempt" to become a singer. Jane's behavioral response following the negative performance outcome (i.e., dropping her head on the desk, bit-ter tears running down her face) is consistent with an experience of shame (Lewis & Sullivan, 2005). She also seemed to hold a fixed mindset about her singing ability (i.e., becoming a singer was now viewed as a *vain attempt*). Finally, Jane seems to have internalized the outcome.

We would further posit that her teacher's feedback and Jane's level of aspiration commitment played moderating roles. Her teacher ridiculed her efforts, which in turn seemed to strongly influence how Jane interpreted and experienced her performance. With respect to aspirational commitment, we would characterize Jane as having a moderate level of commitment (i.e., wanting to become a singer, but with limited experience in the domain). We would therefore assert that her moderate level of aspirational commitment increased her vulnerability to CM. Finally, we would argue that the sociocul-tural context also played a moderating role. Given that the triggering event occurred in a setting to which she would need to return and involved people who represent a legitimate authority (teacher) and peer group (classmates), this likely intensified her feelings of shame and motivated her to abandon her aspiration to become a singer.

Creative Continuance Example. The second example focuses on cre-ative continuance. The highly accomplished composer Steven Sondheim recounted in a 2010 radio interview a key formative experience he had with his mentor Oscar Hammerstein (Alvarez & Howard, 2010). When

Sondheim was 15, he had the creative aspiration to become a show-tune composer. He had written a school musical and asked Hammerstein for feedback. Sondheim wanted a candid critique and therefore asked Hammerstein, "Pretend you don't know me and it had just crossed your desk." In response, Hammerstein said, "well in that case I have to tell you it is the worst thing I have ever read" (Alvarez & Howard, 2010). Clearly, this is a negative performance outcome. If the interaction stopped at this moment, Sondheim may have given up on his creative aspiration.

Instead, Hammerstein provided detailed feedback of how Sondheim could improve the work. As Sondheim explained, "he treated me like an adult and he did it as an encouragement" (Alvarez & Howard, 2010). Sondheim further explained, "he went through it page by page … [and I] probably learned more about song writing for theatre that afternoon than most writers probably learn in a lifetime" (Alvarez & Howard, 2010). We would assert that this detailed, improvement-oriented feedback communicated a growth mindset. Consequently, even if Sondheim did internalize the negative outcome, he was receiving the message that improvement was possible.

Finally, we would assert that although Sondheim's aspirational commitment may have been at a moderate level (making him more vulnerable to CM), the sociocultural context afforded one-on-one coaching and feedback to help buffer him from viewing the situation through the lens of fixed ability beliefs or from feeling the self-conscious hurtful emotion of shame. As Sondheim explained, "it was a disappointment, not a hurt."

Concluding Thoughts

There are various experiences in childhood and adolescence that can influence the development of young people's creative aspirations. In this short article, we have focused on one experience: creative mortification. CM is a subjective affair. It can therefore be quite subtle and occur without notice from others. We have attempted to draw attention to this phenomenon and introduced an empirically testable model that researchers can use to examine the process by which CM seems to occur. The model contributes new insights into how existing motivational and emotional constructs can be used to understand why some young people may abandon their creative aspirations. It thereby highlights potential areas for how researchers and practitioners might further clarify the process and, ultimately, develop ways to help young people avoid or rebound from mortifying experiences.

We recognize that many questions remain. One question worth exploring is whether certain aspects of CM can be adaptive. Leitner, Hehman, Deegan, and Jones (2014) have, for instance, described "adaptive disengagement" as a way to protect one's self-esteem from negative social feedback. Indeed, adaptive disengagement may resolve the dissonance experienced from receiving negative performance-related feedback. On the downside, disengagement may run the risk of the young person becoming unreceptive to helpful, albeit negative, feedback. As such, practitioners play a key role in helping young people learn how to receive and, when necessary, act on feedback associated with negative performance outcomes. Indeed, providing and helping young people learn how to receive *honest* (i.e., understand real-world requirements necessary for creative accomplishment) and *supportive* feedback (i.e., what specifically they can do to improve upon their current level of competence) seems like a viable way to support the development of creative potential (Beghetto, 2007; Beghetto & Kaufman, 2007).

Additional questions in need of empirical exploration include: Are certain developmental time periods (e.g., transition to adolescence) more critical than others with respect to being vulnerable to CM? Do the effects of a particularly intense CM experience generalize to related performance domains (e.g., an intense experience of CM in poetry resulting in avoiding other forms of creative writing)? What personal or environmental factors might help young people better cope with negative performance outcomes and experience them in a more adaptive and positive way? What role might practitioners play in ameliorating the potentially damaging self-beliefs and negative self-evaluative emotions experienced by young people who face setbacks and real-world constraints in pursuit of their creative aspirations? And under what conditions might young people who have experienced CM return to their former aspirations (including learning how to reframe untenable aspirations into creative hobbies or avocations)?

With further testing and refinement of the model introduced herein, researchers will be in a better position to help young people learn and grow from setbacks. In doing so, more young people might realize the benefits of developing creative aspirations into creative identities.

Notes

1. The process model highlights factors asserted to increase the likelihood of CM. We are not asserting that one variable necessarily causes another (e.g., fixed beliefs cause shame). Rather, CM is simply more likely when all the relevant variables are present.

2. Beghetto (2014) found that CM was uniquely predicted by fixed creative ability beliefs (e.g., "Your artistic ability was not sufficient") and the experience of shame (assessed by a measure adapted from Tracy & Robins, 2006).

3. These examples are adapted from examples and discussion presented in Beghetto (2013).

References

Albert, R. S. (1996). Some reasons why childhood creativity often fails to make it past puberty into the real world. In M. A. Runco (Ed.), *New Directions for Child Development: No. 72. Creativity from childhood through adulthood: The developmental issues* (pp. 43–56). San Francisco, CA: Jossey-Bass.

Alvarez, C., & Howard, A. (Producers). (2010, December). Stephen Sondheim: Finishing the hat. *Bookworm*. [Audio podcast]. Retrieved from http://www.kcrw.com/etc/programs/bw/bw101223stephen_sondheim_fin

Bandura, A. (1997). *Self-efficacy: The exercise of control.* New York: Freeman.

Beghetto, R. A. (2007). Ideational code-switching: Walking the talk about supporting student creativity in the classroom. *Roeper Review, 29,* 265–270.

Beghetto, R. A. (2013). *Killing ideas softly? The promise and perils of creativity in the classroom.* Charlotte, NC: Information Age Publishing.

Beghetto, R. A. (2014). Creative mortification: An initial exploration. *Psychology of Aesthetics, Creativity, and the Arts.* doi: 10.1037/a0036618

Beghetto, R. A., & Kaufman, J. C. (2007). Toward a broader conception of creativity: A case for mini-c creativity. *Psychology of Aesthetics, Creativity, and the Arts, 1,* 73–79.

Cianci, A. M., Klein, H. J., & Seijts, G. H. (2010). The effect of negative feedback on tension and subsequent performance: The main and interactive effects of goal content and conscientiousness. *Journal of Applied Psychology, 4,* 618–630.

DeMunn, N. W., & Snow, F. B. (Eds.). (1865). Discouraging attempts to sing. *The Rhode Island Schoolmaster, 11,* 88–89.

Dweck, C. S. (2006). *Mindset: The new psychology of success.* New York: Random House.

Ericsson, K. A. (Ed.). (1996). The road to expert performance: Empirical evidence from the arts and sciences, sports, and games. Mahwah, NJ: Erlbaum.

Finkelstein, S. R., & Fishbach, A. (2011). *The expert's curse: Shifting to negative feedback.* Chicago: University of Chicago, Booth School of Business.

Hidi, S., & Renninger, K. A. (2006). The four-phase model of interest development. *Educational Psychologist, 41,* 111–127.

Hong, E., & Milgram, R. M. (2008). *Preventing talent loss.* New York: Routledge.

Kaufman, J. C., & Beghetto, R. A. (2013). In praise of Clark Kent: Creative metacognition and the importance of teaching kids when (not) to be creative. *Roeper Review, 35,* 155–165.

Krapp, A. (2002). Structural and dynamic aspects of interest development: Theoretical considerations from an ontogenetic perspective. *Learning and Instruction, 12,* 383–409.

Kruger, J., & Dunning, D. (1999). Unskilled and unaware of it: How difficulties in recognizing one's own incompetence lead to inflated self-assessments. *Journal of Personality and Social Psychology, 77,* 1121–1134.

Leitner, J. B., Hehman, E., Deegan, M. P., & Jones, J. M. (2014). Adaptive disengagement buffers self-esteem from negative social feedback. *Personality and Social Psychology Bulletin, 40,* 1435–1450.

Lewis, M., & Sullivan, M. W. (2005). The development of self-conscious emotion. In A. J. Elliot & C. S. Dweck (Eds.), *Handbook of competence and motivation.* New York: Guilford Press.

Scheff, T. J. (2003). Shame in self and society. *Symbolic Interaction, 26,* 239–262.

Sternberg, R. J., & Lubart, T. I. (1995). *Defying the crowd: Cultivating creativity in a culture of conformity.* New York: Free Press.

Tracy, J. L., & Robins, R. W. (2006). Appraisal antecedents of shame and guilt: Support for a theoretical model. *Personality and Social Psychology Bulletin, 32,* 1339–1351.

Weiner, B. (1985). An attributional theory of achievement motivation and emotion. *Psychological Review, 92,* 548–573.

RONALD A. BEGHETTO *is professor of educational psychology at the University of Connecticut.*

ANNA E. DILLEY *is a PhD student at the University of Connecticut. She received her BA and BS from Purdue University.*

Runco, M. A. (2016). Commentary: Overview of developmental perspectives on creativity and the realization of potential. In B. Barbot (Ed.), *Perspectives on creativity development*. New Directions for Child and Adolescent Development, 151, 97–109.

Commentary: Overview of Developmental Perspectives on Creativity and the Realization of Potential

Mark A. Runco

Abstract

The articles in this issue of New Directions for Child and Adolescent Development nicely summarize recent findings about creativity and development. This commentary underscores some of the key ideas and puts them into a larger context (i.e., the corpus of creativity research). It pinpoints areas of agreement (e.g., the need to take both generative and convergent processes into account when examining developmental changes in creative behavior) but balances this with a discussion of concerns. These include (a) problems with the concept of Big C creativity, as it may confound the realization of creative potential, (b) lack of attention given to cultural relativity, and (c) inappropriate testing of divergent thinking. Still, the progress in the research is clear and the fulfillment of creative potentials increasingly likely. © 2016 Wiley Periodicals, Inc.

A great deal has occurred in the 20 years that have elapsed since *New Directions for Child and Adolescent Development* (NDCAD) devoted an issue to creativity development (Runco, 1996). The field has become interdisciplinary (Darbellay, Moody, Sedooka, & Steffen, 2014; Gardner, 1988; Lindauer, 1992) and methodologies have been introduced and refined—the result being a much more rigorous understanding of creativity and its development. This issue of NDCAD offers a good update and explores the new methodologies and advances that have been made in theory and application.

The primary application of creativity research findings is directed to the fulfillment of potential. This may explain some of the enormous attention that is currently being directed to creativity. It is now common knowledge that creative efforts represent the key to innovation, advancement, and even survival. Creative potentials and efforts are vital for health, innovation, and so many forms of progress. Much of the past research has examined the unambiguous creativity of famous luminaries. This makes for good reading and leads to interesting hypotheses, but much of what is learned from the study of unambiguously creative individuals does not apply to the creative potential that is universally shared and perhaps the key defining characteristic of humanity. This special issue suggests that due attention is being shifted toward creative potential. It is about time.

Research has occasionally looked specifically at creative potential (e.g., Albert, 1990; Helson, 1987; MacKinnon, 1965). Indeed, MacKinnon (1965) titled one of his articles "Personality and the Realization of Creative Potential." When he was conducting his research, personality was the typical focus. As a matter of fact, Albert (1990) and Helson (1987) also focused largely on personality as indicator of potential. The articles contained in this special issue show how far we have come. Empirical work still sometimes includes personality, but cognition, affect, judgment, metacognition, attitude, and even brain function related to creative potential are each targeted and measured in today's creativity research. Each is also discussed in the pages that follow. Much is said about how childhood is related to adult creativity as well.

Potential may sound like a risky topic, but it is used in a variety of sciences. Think here of "potential energy" in physics or of the action potential of neurons, which is an electrical-chemical state. That is not to say that there is no risk when studying and investing in creative potential. Indeed, there is no guarantee with potential. If the right conditions are met, potential might be fulfilled, and then there is a payoff. The articles presented in this special issue identify what conditions need to be met in order to fulfill potential. They point to culture and family, and they discuss methods that can be systematically introduced as training. Brain function is brought into the picture, as are immediate environmental conditions, such as those that allow imaginative play.

NEW DIRECTIONS FOR CHILD AND ADOLESCENT DEVELOPMENT • DOI: 10.1002/cad

Longitudinal Research on Creativity

Creativity is now studied with quite varied methods. Russ (Article 2) describes the longitudinal approach. She begins by asking, how does childhood relate to adult creativity? Russ has long investigated play as a critical antecedent to adult creativity (cf. Moore & Russ, 2008; Russ, Robins, & Christiano, 1999; Russ & Schafer, 2006). This line of research is compelling in that it includes both cognition and affect, and because it uses the best methodology for the examination of developmental trajectories, namely the longitudinal design (Albert, 1991; Cramond, Mathews-Morgan, Bandalos, & Zuo, 2005; Csikszentmihalyi, 1990; Harrington, Block, & Block, 1983; Helson, 1999; McCrae, Arenberg, & Costa, 1987; Milgram & Hong, 1999; Runco, 1999; Runco, Millar, Acar, & Cramond, 2011). Russ is quite clear about the limitations of longitudinal research and calls for additional research, preferably from diverse sites and representing diverse samples.

Russ is also clear about why pretend play during childhood is an antecedent of adult creativity. It provides children with practice using fantasy and symbolism. Children can try using one thing as if it was another, solve problems, shift perspectives, integrate affect into cognition. Combinatorial thinking often arises when playing, as does "self-generated thought." Combinatorial and self-generated thought are especially important because they are often used in the neuroscientific research on creativity (Dietrich, 2015).

Self-generated thought may be the least recognized type of cognition in that list, but then again, it is consistent with what Piaget (1976) called *reflective abstraction* in his theory of cognitive development. Cognitive growth is often a matter of adaptation to experience, according to Piaget, and an attempt to resolve disequilibrium, but cognition can also develop as a result of reflective abstraction. This is entirely internal rather than a reaction to an external disequilibrium. Self-generated thinking and reflective abstraction are both noteworthy because they bridge childhood and adult creativity, but also because they assume a particular kind of creative process. Many descriptions look to combinatorial thinking, analogies, and other processes implying that thinking is in fact not all that original. Analogical processes, for example, find a seemingly new idea in existing knowledge. One implication of this is that there is no real originality and that all creative things are based on what already existed. Self-generated thought and reflective abstraction, on the other hand, point to authentic creative insights that are truly new and original. That is significant given that originality is the primary component in virtually all definitions of creativity (Runco & Jaeger, 2012).

Emphasis should also be given to Russ' claim that the rewarding feelings experienced when a child plays are responsible for the lifelong desire to behave creatively. This logic goes a long way toward explaining how childhood is tied to adult creativity. It explains *why*, not just *what*. Adults may explore wide associations, take time with problems, and consider different perspectives and possibilities (i.e., think creatively) because they found, as children, that these activities were enjoyable.

One important methodological implication follows from the fact that Russ (Article 2) and others use divergent thinking (DT) tests. These do provide reliable data about creative potential (Runco, 2013; Torrance, 1995). Yet the idea of play being enjoyable—which was just used to explain why children who have opportunities for imaginative play are creative as adults—should also be remembered whenever tests of DT are used for research. Put briefly, measures of DT are probably not meaningful estimates of creative potential unless they are given in playful, gamelike testing settings. If tests of DT are given in testlike settings, creative children are not very creative. Children (at least over age 7 or 8) assume that the "test" they are taking is like all other tests they have ever taken and, as a result, they will not give original answers. Instead, they will give conventional answers. By age 7 or 8, children have learned that tests are timed, that spelling is important, and that high marks and grades are given only for answers that are conventional. This is a part of socialization and "test wiseness." The result is that only when DT tests are given in playful gamelike settings do they uncover the true creative potentials of children. In playful, gamelike settings, children explore wide associative horizons and consider unconventional and thus original ideas. In testlike settings, children tend to be conventional rather than original, and children who would stand out if given the opportunity to be original behave in an unexceptional and conventional fashion under standard testing conditions.

There are two reasons why creativity tests are often given in testlike rather than gamelike settings. First is a set of expectations that most educators have about tests and about play. For obvious reasons, these parallel the expectations of the 7- and 8-year-old children mentioned. One of these reasons is that, in Western culture, tests are viewed as serious events. Teachers want students to do their best, and that inevitably means, "be serious, don't play around." Related to this, is the cultural view that play is not a serious thing. This view is incorrect. Indeed, businesses would go a long way if they encouraged playful, lighthearted problem solving (March, 1987). When businesses are entirely serious, with no playfulness, many creative ideas are not considered. Much the same applies to the schools.

The second reason is that researchers often forget that there is no such thing as a creativity test. Tests provide only estimates of creative potential. Authentic creative behavior requires spontaneity, so if a student is required to take a test, the result is not really indicative of "creativity." At best, the test provides an estimate of what the student might do, if he or she was intrinsically motivated, spontaneous, and original. Because it is often forgotten that available measures are really only estimates of potential, test scores are sometimes inaccurately viewed as creativity scores. Worse, because available measures of creative potential are called "tests," they are given like other tests, with time limits and constraint—and relatively

NEW DIRECTIONS FOR CHILD AND ADOLESCENT DEVELOPMENT • DOI: 10.1002/cad

meaningless results. More will be said about this, but for now the point is that the more the control, the less likely is the spontaneity, playfulness, intrinsic motivation, and creativity.

DT represents only one component of creative thinking and is by itself not synonymous with creative problem solving. As a matter of fact, antithetical processes also play a role in actual creative performances (Cropley, 2006, 2015; Hoppe & Kyle, 1990; Runco, 2003c). Cassotti, Agogué, Camarda, Houdé, and Borst (Article 5) alluded to a possible complementarity of original thinking with convergent and evaluative processes. They recognize that creativity is more than originality and DT, and that evaluations and judgment are necessary as well. Without some sort of evaluation, ideas are probably almost random, and certainly many of them are worthless. Recall that creativity is more than originality; effectiveness is also required. Evaluative and convergent processes insure this effectiveness. Runco and Charles (1997) and Lubart and Lautrey (1996) both postulated that fourth-grade slump may be a result of maturing logical, convergent, and evaluative processes.

It is quite interesting that Cassotti et al. (Article 5) describe inhibition first and then generation. It is more typical to think about the generation of options and then a selection from among them. Admittedly, the reasoning of Cassotti et al. focuses on a particular kind of creative potential (that which involves insight and intuition) so the relevance to other kinds of creative potential (such as DT) is uncertain. Indeed, there are reasons to suspect that the processes described by Cassotti et al. differ from divergent and original ideation. Cassotti et al. believe that individuals depend on "the most common and accessible knowledge within a specific domain." Runco and Smith (1992) and Runco, Dow, and Smith (2006) demonstrated that original ideation, as assessed with tests of DT, is relatively independent of knowledge and experience. One parallel between the methods cited by Cassotti et al. and those necessary for DT involves fixedness "during the generation of creative ideas may develop with age." This echoes data showing that the flexibility of DT diminishes among older adults (Chown, 1961; Guilford, 1968; Runco & Charles, 1997).

Regardless of age, there can be little doubt that the fulfillment of creative potential depends on the "goodness of fit" between the person and the environment (Runco, 2001). Runco borrowed the idea of "a match" from the developmental literature (e.g., Hunt & Paraskevopoulos, 1980) and described a range of optima that will make it likely that creative potentials are fulfilled. Albert (1978) underscored the need for a match between parents and children. Runco and Sakamoto (1991) described "the problem of the match" that occurs when optimal support for a child's creativity requires parents *scaffold* by making adjustments as the needs of a child change with age. All of this seems to be fairly consistent with the idea from Barbot et al. (Article 3) about the resources that are required for the realization of creative potential.

Barbot et al. (Article 3) and Kornilov, Kornilova, and Grigorenko (Article 4) refer to *Big C creativity*. Their fine work does not hinge on this concept, but it is worth reiterating that this concept should probably be avoided when discussing development and creativity. The high-level creative performances under the umbrella of Big C creativity differ in many ways from what is labeled *little c creativity*. Barbot et al. (Article 3) do an excellent job distinguishing creative achievement from creative potential. That may very well be the most important distinction in the developmental literature when discussing how to support children's creative talents. The problem with Big C is simply that it suggests a false dichotomy (Runco, 2014a; also see Merrotsy, 2013) and is too easily interpreted as if Big C creativity was unconnected to little c creativity. What is really needed, is to avoid the dichotomization so that the continuity of creativity across the life span can be recognized. What separates little c creativity from Big C creativity is personality, knowledge, and opportunity, not really creativity at all. All Big C creators had little c creative potential.

Optimal support for creative potential varies from domain to domain (Barbot et al., Article 3). Still, there is a distinct possibility that there is a general factor ("g") involved in all creative potential and all creative achievements. Runco (1996, 2003b) proposed *the capacity for original interpretations of experience* as a candidate for "g." This follows from the fact that all definitions of creativity, including that offered by Barbot et al., have originality as a prerequisite. Creativity varies from culture to culture, domain to domain, yet originality is a part of a universal capacity to construct meaningful *interpretations of experience*. This is often called an interpretive process, or *top-down processing*, but regardless of the label, it is clear that humans can use experience and do not just memorize. We construct meaning. Frequently, that is personally constructed meaning, and often that personally constructed meaning is original and useful. In that light, the construction of meaningful interpretations satisfies the definition of creativity, at least if the definition does not require social recognition. It is best to exclude social recognition from a definition of creativity, given how much subjectivity that introduces. A definition with social recognition also confounds creativity with fame, influence, and impact (Runco, 1995). There are social influences on the fulfillment of creative potentials, but those are influences and not a part of the actual creative acts. Recognition is a result of creative behavior, not a part of it (Runco, 2011).

The idea of a universal capacity required for all creative behavior may sound contrary to Baer's (Article 1) view of domain-specific knowledge. Note, however, that Baer refers to "creativity." If he had referred to "creative performance," there would be no contradiction between the idea of a universal creative capacity and Baer's view. There is an apparent contradiction, but only because what is universal in creativity is a capacity, which is quite different from creative performance, in that the latter may indeed require domain-specific knowledge. In this light, the single word

NEW DIRECTIONS FOR CHILD AND ADOLESCENT DEVELOPMENT • DOI: 10.1002/cad

"creativity" is probably too ambiguous for discussions of the development of creativity.

The possibility of a universal capacity required for all creative thinking is more clearly contrary to the theory of a creativity complex and suggests that care must be taken when examining peaks, slumps, and discontinuities in the development of creativity. The evidence reviewed by Barbot et al. (Article 3; cf. Runco & Charles, 1997) is certain that creative performance, be it on a test of DT or some sort of socially recognized creative achievement, will show discontinuities, but there is still a good possibility that the universal creative capacity (i.e., the ability to construct original interpretations of experience) is continuous across the life span, at least until neurological changes inhibit brain function late in life. The idea of a continuous, unitary, universal creative capacity does not detract from the impact relevant resources will have on development, nor does it change the need for optimization of supports for creativity (Barbot et al., Article 3; Runco & Gaynor, 1993).

Any discussion of what is universal and what is not universal must recognize culture. Culture has received attention in the research of the past 20 years (Kharkhurin, 2014; Rudowicz & Yue, 2002; Runco, 2004, 2014b, chapter 8; Tan, in press). In the present issue of NDCAD, Kornilov, Kornilova, and Grigorenko (Article 4) and Beghetto and Dilley (Article 7) say much about creativity developing within sociocultural context. Beghetto and Dilley detail the formation of identity and the role it plays in the creative process. Kornilov et al. suggest that "cultures have been found to differ with respect to the relative emphasis that they place on specific characteristics" and that creativity depends on "cultural expectations regarding what is considered creative and why." Expectations were mentioned earlier in this commentary. Beghetto and Dilley (Article 7) underscore self-attributions, a special case of expectations, in their explanation of how a creative identity might not survive into adulthood. All of this fits with Kharkhurin's (2014) reasoning that creative behavior in many cultures requires authenticity, in addition to originality and usefulness.

Kornilov et al. point to family environment, which is important because the cultural values that influence creative development are communicated to children through the family (Albert & Runco, 1989), along with education (Runco, 2003b). Of course, any time the family is a factor it is likely that both shared genes and shared experiences and values are involved. Genetics represents one of the additions to the interdisciplinarity discussed earlier in this commentary (Murphy, Runco, Acar, & Reiter-Palmon, 2013).

Concerns and Conclusions

The articles in this issue of NDCAD nicely summarize recent findings about creativity and development. The individual authors and research teams do an admirable job of presenting the new findings. This commentary underscored some of the key ideas and put them into a larger context (i.e., the corpus of creativity research). A commentary should offer a balanced view, which is why the false dichotomy of Big C vs. little c was mentioned. Another concern involved the possibility that creativity is not entirely domain specific, but may be in part a function of a universal human capacity for constructing interpretations.

There are several methodological concerns. Some of these are reactions specifically to the research using DT. It is gratifying to see that DT is finally being examined in neuroscientific research and the work of Kleibeuker, Koolschijn, Jolles, De Dreu, and Crone (2013) and Kleibeuker, De Dreu, and Crone (Article 6). So many functional magnetic resonance imaging (fMRI) studies focus on insight, which is not as clearly tied to the originality that is a part of all creativity. DT tests are imperfect, but (a) they have a clear theoretical tie to creativity, and the theory is detailed, parsimonious, and testable, and (b) so much research has been done on DT that we are well aware of the limitations and appropriate uses.

That does take us to one methodological concern, namely that DT is not being measured as it should be, as dictated by years of research (e.g., Guilford, 1968; Runco, 1986, 1999, 2013; Torrance, 1995; Wallach & Kogan, 1965). In some research, only one task is used. This may not sound like a problem, but I mean one task, not one test. Using just one item for DT is like testing IQ with a single question or like awarding a grade to a student, after a full year of instruction, based on an answer to one question. Psychometric theory indicates that short tests are less reliable than long tests, and of course the nominal case is a single-item test. For this reason, good research on DT has always used multiple tests rather than a single test. Wallach and Kogan (1965), for example, had five tests, each with at least three tasks. This is quite important because a reliable test has a small amount of measurement error. You can't even estimate this kind of error if only one item is given.

A related concern involves subjective ratings when scoring DT tests. This too is contrary to decades of research on DT (e.g., Guilford and the others cited previously). The objective scoring of DT, including originality and flexibility, was refined in quite a number of investigations. This is one of the primary attractions of DT tests. They allow objective determination of originality! Ideas can be rated subjectively instead, and several studies have compared objective and subjective scores (e.g., Hocevar, 1979; Runco, Okuda, & Thurston, 1987). The subjective scores are often reliable, but it is not the same kind of reliability as is provided by measures of internal consistency, and looking specifically at internal consistency has distinct advantages. In addition, evidence suggests that ratings from one group of judges do not correlate with ratings from other groups (Runco, 1989; Runco, McCarthy, & Svensen, 1994).

One last methodological issue concerns time limits. The theoretical bases for DT (Guilford, 1968; Mednick, 1962; Wallach & Kogan, 1965) are based on an underlying process that requires time for the discovery or construction of original ideas. The need for time has been repeatedly supported (e.g., Mednick, 1962; Milgram & Rabkin, 1980; Runco, 1986). There is a recent study or two suggesting that time is not as important as early data suggested, but these recent data ignore theory and the same methodological requirements mentioned earlier (e.g., objective scoring, reliable tests). Recall also at this point what Russ (Article 2) said about the value of play: it allows wide associative horizons and is conducive to creative thinking. Play, like DT, should not be rushed. This is why the testing of DT that provides the most reliable scores uses gamelike rather than testlike conditions.

There are actually two problems when DT tests are timed. First, it takes time to move from idea to idea. Without adequate time, examinees rely on memory and rote ideation, which would imply that timed tests tell us more about memory and experience and not about DT and creativity. The second problem is that when examinees know they are being timed, they tend to assume that the test is a convergent one, like they received in school, and thus they tend to think convergently instead of divergently. They are not original. This indicates that examinees might be given a large amount of time, but if they know they are being timed, they still will not be original and creative. To allow original thinking and to ensure that the gamelike nature of the testing setting is obvious to examinees, they should be told something like, "take your time," "you have as much time as you like." Without this sort of thing, it is quite possible that, even if the task at hand is from a DT test, the ideas given by examinees will not be indicative of their creative potential.

These suggestions for accurate testing fit well with research on settings and climates that support the expression of creativity (Amabile & Gryskiewicz, 1989; Harrington, Block, & Block, 1987). Harrington et al. (1987) described the benefits of Rogerian and supportive homes for the development of creativity. There is, then, a theme in the creativity research. This is particularly meaningful in that it complements research on the creative process and the creative personality. The theme can be summarized: *The creative process involves originality, spontaneity, wide associations, and authenticity, and environments that are designed to support creativity should allow each of these.* That applies to schools, the home, organizations, and even testing settings.

The articles in this volume recognize that creative capacities change, and not just during childhood. Kleibeuker, De Dreu, and Crone (Article 6) focus on adolescent creativity, which is fortunate because there are important changes occurring in the adolescent brain. Kleibeuker et al.'s work is very practical, given their extensive training program. Perhaps this training could be used along with other effective programs, including that which focuses on DT and strategic thinking (Runco, Illies, & Eisenman, 2005; Runco, Illies, & Reiter-Palmon, 2005). Beghetto and Dilley (Article 7) also offered an optimistic view of creative development when they turned possible squelchers of creativity into a recipe for continued growth (e.g., "externalize failure, hold growth beliefs, and do not feel shamed by negative performance outcomes").

Future research should continue to explore the antecedents to creativity and the realization of potential. There is a great deal to be done on the topic of creativity and development, but this special issue represents a step forward. No other talent promises such huge payoffs as creativity. If creative potential can be clearly defined and measured, the world will be a better place.

References

Albert, R. S. (1978). Observations and suggestions regarding giftedness, familial influence and the achievement of eminence. *Gifted Child Quarterly, 22,* 201–211.

Albert, R. S. (1990). Identify, experiences, and career choice among the exceptionally gifted and eminent. In M. A. Runco & R. S. Albert (Eds.), *Theories of creativity* (pp. 11–34). Newbury Park, CA: Sage.

Albert, R. S. (1991). People, processes, and developmental paths to eminence: A developmental-interactional model. In R. M. Milgram (Ed.), *Counseling gifted and talented children* (pp. 75–93). Norwood, NJ: Ablex.

Albert, R. S., & Runco, M. A. (1989). Independence and cognitive ability in gifted and exceptionally gifted boys. *Journal of Youth and Adolescence, 18,* 221–230.

Amabile, T.M., & Gryskiewicz, N.D. (1989). The creative environment scales: Work environment inventory. *Creativity Research Journal, 2,* 231–253.

Chown, S. M. (1961). Age and the rigidities. *Journal of Gerontology, 16,* 353–362.

Cramond, B., Mathews-Morgan, J. Bandalos, D., & Zuo, L. (2005). A report on the 40-year follow-up of the Torrance Tests of Creative Thinking: Alive and well in the new millennium. *Gifted Child Quarterly, 49,* 283–291.

Cropley, A. J. (2006). In praise of convergent thinking. *Creativity Research Journal, 18*(3), 391–404.

Cropley, A. J. (2015). *Transferable criteria of creativity: A universal aesthetic.* Presented at the New Zealand Creativity Challenge: Creativity crosses boundaries, Wellington, NZ. doi: 10.13140/RG.2.1.2784.3283

Csikszentmihalyi, M. (1990). The domain of creativity. In M. A. Runco & R. S. Albert (Eds.), *Theories of creativity* (pp. 190–212). Newbury Park: Sage.

Dietrich, A. (2015). *How creativity happens in the brain.* London: Palgrave Macmillan.

Darbellay, F., Moody, Z., Sedooka, A., & Steffen, G. (2014). Interdisciplinary research boosted by serendipity. *Creativity Research Journal, 26,* 1–10.

Gardner, H. (1988). Creativity: An interdisciplinary perspective. *Creativity Research Journal, 1,* 8–26.

Guilford, J. P. (1968). *Creativity, intelligence and their educational implications.* San Diego, CA: EDITS/Knapp.

Harrington, D. M., Block, J., & Block, J. H. (1983). Predicting creativity in preadolescence form DT in early childhood. *Journal of Personality and Social Psychology, 45,* 609–623.

Harrington, D. M., Block, J. H., & Block, J. (1987). Testing aspects of Carl Rogers' theory of creative environments: Child-rearing antecedents of creative potential in young adolescents. *Journal of Personality and Social Psychology, 52,* 851–856.

Helson, R. (1987). Which of those women with creative potential became creative? In R. Hogan & W. H. Jones (Eds.), *Perspectives in personality* (Vol. 2, pp. 51–92). Greenwich, CT: JAI.

Helson, R. (1999). A longitudinal study of creative personality in women. *Creativity Research Journal, 12*, 89–102.

Hocevar, D. (1979). A comparison of statistical infrequency and subjective judgment as criteria in the measurement of originality. *Journal of Personality Assessment, 43*, 297–299.

Hoppe, K. D., & Kyle, N. L. (1990). Dual brain, creativity, and health. *Creativity Research Journal, 3*, 150–157.

Hunt, J. McV., & Paraskevopoulos, J. (1980). Children's psychological development as a function of the inaccuracy of their mothers' knowledge of their abilities. *Journal of Genetic Psychology, 136*, 285–298.

Kharkhurin, A. V. (2014). Creativity four-in-one: Four criterion construct of creativity. *Creativity Research Journal, 26*, 338–352.

Kleibeuker, S. W., Koolschijn, P. C. M. P., Jolles, D. D., de Dreu, C. K. W., & Crone, E. A. (2013). The neural coding of creative idea generation across adolescence and early adulthood. *Frontiers in Human Neuroscience, 7*, 905. doi:10.3389/fnhum.2013.00905

Lindauer, M. S. (1992). Creativity in aging artists: Contributions from the humanities to the psychology of aging. *Creativity Research Journal, 5*, 211–232.

Lubart, T., Lautrey, J. (1996). Development of creativity in 9- to 10-year old children. Presented at the Growing Mind Conference, Geneva, Switzerland.

MacKinnon, D. (1965). Personality and the realization of creative potential. *American Psychologist, 20*, 273–281.

March, J. G. (1987). The technology of foolishness. In J. G. March & J. P. Olsen (Eds.), *Ambiguity and choice in organizations* (pp. 69–81). Bergen, Norway: Universitets-Forlaget.

McCrae, R. R., Arenberg, D., & Costa, P. T., Jr. (1987). Declines in divergent thinking with age: Cross-sectional, longitudinal, and cross-sequential analyses. *Psychology and Aging, 2*, 130–137.

Mednick, S. (1962). The associative basis of the creative process. *Psychological Review, 69*, 220–232.

Merrotsy, P. (2013). A note on Big-C Creativity and little-c creativity. *Creativity Research Journal, 25*(4), 474–476.

Milgram, R. M., & Hong, E. (1999). Creative out-of-school activities in intellectually gifted adolescents as predictors of their life accomplishments in young adults: A longitudinal study. *Creativity Research Journal, 12*, 77–88.

Milgram, R. M., & Rabkin, L. (1980). Developmental test of Mednick's associative hierarchies of original thinking. *Developmental Psychology, 16*, 157–158.

Moore, M., & Russ, S. (2008). Follow-up of a pretend play intervention: Effects on play, creativity, and emotional processes in children. *Creativity Research Journal, 20*, 427–436.

Murphy, M., Runco, M. A., Acar, S., & Reiter-Palmon, R. (2013). Reanalysis of genetic data and rethinking dopamine's relationship with creativity. *Creativity Research Journal, 25*, 147–148.

Piaget, J. (1976). *To understand is to invent.* New York: Penguin.

Rudowicz, E. & Yue, X. D. (2002). Compatibility of Chinese and creative personalities. *Creativity Research Journal, 14*(3), 387–394.

Runco, M. A. (1986). Flexibility and originality in children's divergent thinking. *Journal of Psychology, 120*, 345–352.

Runco, M. A. (1989). The creativity of children's art. *Child Study Journal, 19*, 177–189.

Runco, M. A. (1995). Insight for creativity, expression for impact. *Creativity Research Journal, 8*, 377–390.

Runco, M. A. (1996). Personal creativity: Definition and developmental issues. In *New Directions for Child Development: No.72. Creativity from childhood through adulthood: The developmental issues* (pp. 3–30). San Francisco, CA: Jossey-Bass.

Runco, M. A. (Ed.). (1999). Longitudinal studies of creativity: Special issue of the *Creativity Research Journal*. *Creativity Research Journal, 12* [whole issue].

Runco, M. A. (2001). Creativity as optimal human functioning. In M. Bloom (Ed.), *Promoting creativity across the lifespan* (pp. 17–44). Washington, DC: Child Welfare League of America.

Runco, M. A. (2003a). (Ed.). *Critical creative processes*. Cresskill, NJ: Hampton Press.

Runco, M. A. (2003b). Education for creative potential. *Scandinavian Journal of Education, 47*, 317–324.

Runco, M. A. (2003c). Idea evaluation, divergent thinking, and creativity. In M. A. Runco (Ed.), *Critical creative processes* (pp. 69–94). Cresskill, NJ: Hampton Press.

Runco, M. A. (2004). Personal creativity and culture. In L. Sing, A. N. N. Hui, & G. C. Ng (Eds.), *Creativity: When East meets West* (pp. 9–21). Singapore: World Scientific Publishing.

Runco, M. A. (2011). Personal creativity. In M. A. Runco & S. Pritzker (Eds.), *Encyclopedia of creativity* (2nd ed., pp. 220–223). San Diego, CA: Elsevier.

Runco, M. A. (Ed.). (2013). *Divergent thinking and creative potential*. Cresskill, NJ: Hampton Press.

Runco, M. A. (2014a). "Big C, little c" creativity as a false dichotomy: Reality is not categorical. *Creativity Research Journal, 26*, 131–132.

Runco, M. A. (2014b). *Creativity: Theories and themes: Research, development, and practice* (rev. ed.). San Diego, CA: Academic Press.

Runco, M. A., & Charles, R. E. (1997). Developmental trends in creative potential and creative performance. In M. A. Runco (Ed.), *The creativity research handbook* (Vol. 1, pp. 115–152). Cresskill, NJ: Hampton Press.

Runco, M. A., Dow, G., & Smith, W. R. (2006). Information, experience, divergent thinking: An empirical test. *Creativity Research Journal, 18*(3), 269–277.

Runco, M. A., & Gaynor J. L. R. (1993). Creativity as optimal development. In J. Brzezinski, S. DiNuovo, T. Marek, & T. Maruszewski (Eds.), *Creativity and consciousness: Philosophical and psychological dimensions* (pp. 395–412). Amsterdam/Atlanta: Rodopi.

Runco, M. A., Illies, J.J. , & Eisenman, R. (2005). Creativity, originality, and appropriateness: What do explicit instructions tell us about their relationships? *Journal of Creative Behavior, 39*, 137–148.

Runco, M. A., Illies, J. J., & Reiter-Palmon, R. (2005). Explicit instructions to be creative and original: A comparison of strategies and criteria as targets with three types of divergent thinking tests. *Korean Journal of Thinking and Problem Solving, 15*, 5–15.

Runco, M. A., & Jaeger, G. (2012). The standard definition of creativity. *Creativity Research Journal, 24*, 92–96.

Runco, M. A., McCarthy, K. A., & Svensen, E. (1994). Judgments of the creativity of artwork from students and professional artists. *Journal of Psychology, 128*, 23–31.

Runco, M. A., Millar, G., Acar, S., Cramond, B. (2011). Torrance tests of creative thinking as predictors of personal and public achievement: A fifty year follow-up. *Creativity Research Journal, 22*, 361–368.

Runco, M. A., Okuda, S. M., & Thurston, B. J. (1987). The psychometric properties of four systems for scoring divergent thinking tests. *Journal of Psychoeducational Assessment, 5*, 149–156.

Runco, M. A., & Sakamoto, S. O. (1991). Optimization as a guiding principle in research on creative problem solving. In T. Helstrup, G. Kaufmann, & K. H. Teigen (Eds.), *Problem solving and cognitive processes: Essays in honor of Kjell Raaheim* (pp. 119–144). Bergen, Norway: Fagbokforlaget Vigmostad & Bjorke.

Runco, M. A., & Smith, W. R. (1992). Interpersonal and intrapersonal evaluations of creative ideas. *Personality and Individual Differences, 13*, 295–302.

Russ, S. W., Robins, A., & Christiano, B. (1999). Pretend play: longitudinal prediction of creativity and affect in fantasy in children. *Creativity Research Journal, 12*, 129–139.

Russ, S. W., & Schafer, E. (2006). Affect in fantasy play, emotion in memories and divergent thinking. *Creativity Research Journal, 18*, 347–354.

Tan, C. (in press). Creativity and Confucius. *Journal of Genius and Eminence.*

Torrance, E. P. (1995). *Why fly?* Norwood, NJ: Ablex.

Wallach, M. A., & Kogan, N. (1965). *Modes of thinking in young children: A study of the creativity-intelligence distinction.* New York: Holt, Reinhart, & Winston.

MARK A. RUNCO is the Distinguished Research Fellow for the American Institute of Behavioral Research & Technology and professor at the University of Georgia, Athens, GA, USA.

Silvia, P. J., Christensen, A. P., & Cotter, K. N. (2016). Commentary: The development of creativity—ability, motivation, and potential. In B. Barbot (Ed.), *Perspectives on creativity development. New Directions for Child and Adolescent Development, 151*, 111–119.

Commentary: The Development of Creativity—Ability, Motivation, and Potential

Paul J. Silvia, Alexander P. Christensen, Katherine N. Cotter

Abstract

A major question for research on the development of creativity is whether it is interested in creative potential (a prospective approach that uses measures early in life to predict adult creativity) or in children's creativity for its own sake. We suggest that a focus on potential for future creativity diminishes the fascinating creative world of childhood. The contributions to this issue can be organized in light of an ability × motivation framework, which offers a fruitful way for thinking about the many factors that foster and impede creativity. The contributions reflect a renewed interest in the development of creativity and highlight how this area can illuminate broader problems in creativity studies. © 2016 Wiley Periodicals, Inc.

C reativity science attracts, shall we say, a certain sort of researcher—someone relatively high in openness to experience, interested in the arts, and willing to stand out. Because it attracts researchers interested in novelty and innovation, creativity research is unusually heterogeneous. We certainly see that diversity in this collection of contributions, which cover an unusually broad range of samples, constructs, methods, and approaches to creativity and its development. As researchers who study adults, we're happy for the opportunity to reflect on these articles and the broader problem of the development of creativity. In this commentary, we raise some general issues that cut across these articles and consider a general framework that might organize the many factors that contribute to the development of creativity.

What Develops? Creative Potential or Creativity?

What develops in the development of creativity: *creative potential* or *creativity?* These terms tend to be used interchangeably, especially in discussions of creative thought and divergent thinking (DT), but each term is freighted with tacit meanings that shape how we study creativity's development.

When we emphasize *creative potential*, we take a future-oriented view of a child's creative actions. Processes like pretend play or divergent thinking, when viewed as measures of creative potential, are interesting because they predict creative behaviors later in the life span. What we assess in childhood isn't creativity *per se* but rather some indicator that predicts future creative accomplishments. Runco (2014) has probably developed the view of creative potential most thoroughly. In his writings, he has argued that DT tests measure creative potential, not creativity. Runco and Acar (2012), for example, conclude that "DT tests are not tests of creativity. They are estimates of the potential for creative problem solving" (p. 72).

Focusing on creative potential shifts the goals of research and intervention. If we are interested in potential, then our eyes are looking down the road. We are studying children, for example, but our evidence for validity comes from studying what these children do later on as teens and grown-ups. The criterion for validity for measures of creative potential are necessarily prospective: if DT tasks didn't predict later creative achievement, for example, they would have clearly failed as a measure of creative potential. Likewise, the aims of creativity-enhancing interventions shift. If we seek to improve a child's creative potential, then our outcome metrics are measures of future, not current, creativity.

Alternatively, we can study the development of creativity itself. Creativity clearly means many things, but when contrasted with creative potential, it is present oriented instead of future oriented. It emphasizes what people—be they little kids, teens, or grown-ups—are doing and thinking *right now*. This changes the complexion of research and intervention. First, evidence for criterion validity is no longer necessarily prospective. If we are studying how children generate clever ideas for its own sake—not as a measure of their potential to do so as adults—then it is irrelevant if scores on that task predict later achievements. It would be noteworthy if they did, but it wouldn't matter if they didn't. Second, an intervention for creativity—as opposed to creative potential—would be interested in what changes now instead of down the road.

And finally, a focus on creativity, instead of creative potential, includes a wider range of interesting outcomes, not merely public, observable creative accomplishments. Researchers interested in *everyday creativity* and mundane creative acts—the sorts of "little c" creative things people do in everyday life, such as dabbling with musical instruments, scrapbooking, fiddling around with recipes, or making cat memes—point out how much we miss when we emphasize genius, eminence, and achievement (Conner & Silvia, 2015; Kaufman & Beghetto, 2009; Silvia et al., 2014). Focusing on fame, achievement, and accomplishment is perhaps an American thing, but most of the creativity that happens—and perhaps the acts that say the most about people's basic creative natures (Richards, 2007, 2010)—are the more humble daily acts of the silent creative majority.

Our impression is that bickering over whether a task is a measure of *creativity* or *creative potential* is fruitless and misses much of the point of psychological assessment. Executive functioning tests, for example, strongly predict things like later earnings, incarceration, and the number of car accidents someone will go on to cause (Deary, 2001), but we don't commonly call an intelligence test a measure of "earnings potential" or "incarceration potential" or "car accident causing potential."

Test scores can be more or less valid for a wide range of research purposes (Messick, 1995): one's purpose might be using a DT task to understand how children play with ideas, or one might use the scores to forecast later public accomplishment. Validity isn't one thing, and fixating on future achievement as the most important marker of "criterion validity" promotes a limiting conception of validity and assessment. A task could be used as a tool to understand how people come up with good ideas; it could also be used to predict other variables, including ones yet to be measured.

Conceptually, however, the distinction between creativity and creative potential matters, particularly when we consider interventions and creativity training. In some sense, the everyday creative acts of childhood are diminished when adults view them through the lens of future value and achievement. We don't want to be misunderstood: predicting later creativity from childhood constructs is valuable and fascinating. But it would be a shame if the captivating world of childhood creativity were viewed as merely a preparatory period for the big leagues of adult creativity. Children surely don't view their drawing and building and playing and imagining that way.

An Ability × Motivation Framework for the Development of Creativity

A general model of creativity can help us wrap our brains around the diversity of thought surrounding creativity's development. The many ideas tackled in these contributions can be fruitfully nested within an *ability × motivation* framework. Ability and motivation loom large in many theories of creativity, particularly systems, componential, and sociocultural theories (e.g., Amabile, 1996; Sawyer, 2012; Sternberg, 2006). Factors related to *ability* include traits, knowledge, skills, and environmental affordances that can foster or impede the capacity for creative work; factors related to *motivation* include goals, self-regulatory processes, and experiences that foster or impede wanting to invest time in creative activities.

Ability. Many of the ideas developed in these contributions concern abilities: personality traits, cognitive abilities, and acquired skills and knowledge that afford exercising creativity. The study of cognitive abilities has had a renaissance in creativity studies (see Silvia, 2015, for a review), and several of the contributions examine it. Until recently, divergent and convergent thinking were seen as unique and unrelated strengths—most of the textbooks either omitted intelligence or described why it has little to do with creativity. An example of the changing times is the article by Cassotti, Agogué, Camarda, Houdé, and Borst (Article 5), which proposes that inhibitory abilities are central to creative thought in childhood. This takes the study of cognitive abilities and creativity full circle. The debate started in earnest with two landmark studies of childhood creativity (Getzels & Jackson, 1962; Wallach & Kogan, 1965), both of which found that measures of intelligence and creativity were essentially unrelated. Cassotti et al. (Article 5) raise some strong arguments for why the ability to manage your mind is useful for generating, evaluating, and refining ideas, even at early ages. In recent years, research with adult samples has found that many intellectual variables aid in creative thought (see Silvia, 2015), so extending this approach to creative cognition in childhood would be fruitful.

Kleibeuker, De Dreu, and Crone (Article 6) expand on this problem by exploring later age ranges and by considering the neuroscience of creativity's development. It's hard to understate the dramatic quality of brain development across the life span, and their emphasis on how brain development influences creative growth deserves much more attention. The neuroscience of creativity is flourishing, but for practical reasons, nearly all studies recruit adults. Illuminating the connections between brain and the development of creativity—particularly the growth of abilities associated with executive control—would also illuminate some more general problems in the neuroscience of creativity.

Most of developmental neuroscience has focused on individual activated regions of the brain. Neural activity in a specific region, the prefrontal cortex, has shown significant changes throughout childhood and adolescence that correspond to increased executive control and creative ability (Kleibeuker et al., Article 6). Whereas developmental research has concentrated on an individual regions, approach, adult studies have examined local and global interactions via models of brain networks (Jung, 2014). This technique not only gleans information from specific regions but also gives insight into the operation of large-scale networks, such as the default mode network, the salience network, and the executive control network (Andrews-Hanna, 2012; Beaty et al., 2014; Jung, 2014). Studies using this method have shown creative processes are much more complex than previously thought, congruent with the neuroimaging evidence discussed in this issue (Cassotti et al., Article 5; Kleibeuker et al., Article 6). Emphasizing the integration and interaction of individual areas in the form of networks, as well as how different networks in turn interact, greatly expands the scope of creativity neuroscience (Beaty, Benedek, Silvia, & Schacter, 2016). In adult studies, for example, creative thought involves the coupling of the default mode network and the executive control network, two networks that are often negatively related (e.g., Beaty, Benedek, Kaufman, & Silvia, 2015). Although more difficult in children (Kim et al., 2016), network models of creative cognition offer an intriguing avenue for future work in the neuroscience of creativity development.

One promising direction is to examine how changes in semantic network structures affect creativity across development. Recent research on semantic networks shows the structure of knowledge influences idea generation and constrains the effects of other cognitive abilities on creative thought (Kenett, Anaki, & Faust, 2014). Strong executive and inhibitory abilities clearly help, but the way the raw materials are organized matters as well. Given how quickly language and knowledge develop in childhood, it would be fascinating to examine how semantic knowledge organization affects children's creative thinking.

Motivation. The contributions illustrate several of the most important motivational factors in creativity. Russ (Article 2) provides a snapshot of her long-standing research program in pretend play. This is a landmark line of research in the study of the development of creativity, for it raises provocative issues about the creative lives of children and how creativity can be encouraged. We see pretend play as nested within the motivation category for a couple of reasons. For one, the ubiquity of pretend play says much about the creative passion of children. Moreover, individual differences in pretend play likely reflect broader motivational variables that persist across the life span. As researchers who study adults, when we see variation in using one's imagination, improvising new meanings for common objects, and constructing creative worlds, characters, and stories, we think of *openness to experience*, one of the major cross-cultural factors of personality (McCrae & Sutin, 2009). Personality assessment in early childhood is a tricky thing, but individual differences in pretend play must surely be a marker of openness to experience in early childhood. People high in openness to experience, among other things, value creativity more, see themselves as creative people, and seek out chances to do things differently (Kaufman, 2013).

On the other side, we see how creative goals are stunted and discouraged, if not killed outright. The recent concept of *creative mortification* (Beghetto, 2014) is an intriguing new direction for creativity research. Beghetto and Dilley (Article 7) summarize the theory and outline some fertile directions for future research. Models for improving creativity, not surprisingly, focus on how to elevate creativity. But from a motivation perspective, removing barriers that stunt and thwart creativity is just as important—sometimes getting out of the way is just as important as nudging someone forward. Viewed practically, "doing no harm" would be a good starting point for educators, mentors, and parents concerned about fostering creativity in children. In any case, research on who becomes discouraged and who becomes resilient in the face of critical feedback is sorely needed.

Both Ability and Motivation. And, of course, many of the ideas presented in these articles involve both ability and motivation. Baer's (Article 1) emphasis on the importance of specific domains, for example, straddles both. Baer points out that creativity happens within specific—and occasionally idiosyncratic—domains of creativity. Attempts to train or teach for creativity are more likely to work if the creative domain appeals to the child. As a result, educational interventions have to respect and grapple with the variety of creative preferences children have—including some children's relative lack of interest in creative pursuits. At the same time, interest and ability in domains are linked. Vocational interest researchers, for example, have illustrated how people's self-efficacy for a career affects their interest and motivation (Lent, Brown, & Hackett, 1994). When people feel more capable of succeeding in a career, they find it more appealing and interesting. Notably, vocational interest research is domain specific—a core assumption is that the world of work is differentiated, and people need to find a spot where they fit.

Speaking of fit, Barbot, Lubart, and Besançon (Article 3) describe an emerging global model of creativity that promises to reshape research on children's creative trajectories. The "fourth-grade slump" was one of the most intriguing findings in Torrance's influential research program, but it's clear that this trajectory fails to capture the complexity of creative growth. Thinking of creativity in terms of optimality—of personal resources, task features, and environments—is both theoretically useful and surprisingly practical, so this is a model that creativity researchers should keep an eye on. When we consider optimal fit between people and their environments, we can see the need for a more expansive understanding of creative environment. Some can clearly nurture creativity, and others can crush it (Beghetto & Dilley, Article 7), but what about environments that are merely mediocre,

New Directions for Child and Adolescent Development • DOI: 10.1002/cad

that fail to mesh with or engage students' creative aptitudes? Do these evoke a sort of "creative drift"? Will people seek out more congenial environments or try to modify their environments to improve the fit with their aptitudes?

Culture, too, is an issue that straddles ability and motivation. The role of culture in creativity is so vast that we barely know where to start. One place, suggested by Kornilov, Kornilova, and Grigorenko (Article 4), is to tackle the assessment issues involved in work that crosses cultures, borders, and languages. The authors offer some cautionary tales and illustrate some useful tools for tackling the seemingly simple problem of assessing creative writing in two cultures. If aspects of raters aren't controlled, one could easily find specious differences between two cultures, be they mean differences in creative performance or structural differences in how constructs are constituted and assessed.

So, given all these influences, it's no surprise that training for creativity is not as simple as some may think. Once the many factors that influence creativity are recognized, it becomes apparent that a general, catch-all approach to training for creativity will not be effective—it must be specific to the situation at hand (Baer, Article 1). And this type of training need not be relegated to the stereotypical creative domains: many areas could benefit from creativity training. Take, for instance, engineering education. Many programs focus on its technical aspects and theoretical concepts instead of developing creativity (Cropley, 2015). This emphasis could be for a number of reasons, such as not realizing the value of creativity, but it could also result from the complexity of effectively training for creativity in this domain. It is easy to see how a training program asking students to generate novel but impractical ideas would be off-putting to engineering educators—that is not what their field values. It quickly becomes apparent that these creativity training programs must be tailored to their audience. Training for creativity—something that, if done well, could add new dimensions to creativity development—needs a domain-specific makeover.

Conclusion

Several of the contributors pointed out factors that slow the growth of knowledge about the development of creativity. Developmental research—especially longitudinal research—is slow, expensive, and intricate. Research with children can be particularly vexing: they won't sit still for hours of surveys and brain scans. It is thus nice to see an expanding interest in creativity and its development. The creative lives of children are fascinating—both as hints of adult creativity but primarily as objects of fascination in their own right. All of creativity science's major problems come together in the study of creativity's development, so it offers lessons that are particular to development and that are general to all of our field's concern. We're more than a little curious to see how this field itself develops.

Author Note

This commentary was supported by grant RFP-15-12 from the Imagination Institute (www.imagination-institute.org), funded by the John Templeton Foundation. The opinions expressed in this publication are those of the authors and do not necessarily reflect the view of the Imagination Institute or the John Templeton Foundation.

References

Amabile, T. M. (1996). *Creativity in context*. Boulder, CO: Westview.

Andrews-Hanna, J. R. (2012). The brain's default network and its adaptive role in internal mentation. *Neuroscientist, 18*, 251–270.

Beaty, R. E., Benedek, M., Kaufman, S. B., & Silvia, P. J. (2015). Default and executive network coupling supports creative idea production. *Scientific Reports, 5*, 10964. doi: 10.1038/srep10964

Beaty, R. E., Benedek, M., Silvia, P. J., & Schacter, D. L. (2016). Creative cognition and brain network dynamics. *Trends in Cognitive Sciences, 20*(2), 87–95.

Beaty, R. E., Benedek, M., Wilkins, R. W., Jauk, E., Fink, A., Silvia, P. J., et al. (2014). Creativity and the default network: A functional connectivity analysis of the creative brain at rest. *Neuropsychologia, 64*, 92–98.

Beghetto, R. A. (2014). Creative mortification: An initial exploration. *Psychology of Aesthetics, Creativity, and the Arts, 8*, 266–276.

Conner, T. S., & Silvia, P. J. (2015). Creative days: A daily diary study of emotion, personality, and everyday creativity. *Psychology of Aesthetics, Creativity, and the Arts, 9*, 463–470.

Cropley, D. H. (2015). Promoting creativity and innovation in engineering education. *Psychology of Aesthetics, Creativity, and the Arts, 9*, 161–171.

Deary, I. J. (2001). *Intelligence: A very short introduction*. New York, NY: Oxford University Press.

Getzels, J. W., & Jackson, P. W. (1962). *Creativity and intelligence: Explorations with gifted students*. New York: John Wiley.

Jung, R. E. (2014). Evolution, creativity, intelligence, and madness: "Here be dragons." *Frontiers in Psychology, 5*(784), 1–3. doi: 10.3389/fpsyg.2014.00784

Kaufman, S. B. (2013). Opening up openness to experience: A four-factor model and relations to creative achievement in the arts and sciences. *Journal of Creative Behavior, 47*, 233–255.

Kaufman, J. C., & Beghetto, R. A. (2009). Beyond big and little: The four c model of creativity. *Review of General Psychology, 13*, 1–12.

Kenett, Y. N., Anaki, D., & Faust, M. (2014). Investigating the structure of semantic networks in low and high creative persons. *Frontiers in Human Neuroscience, 8*(407), 1–16.

Kim, D. J., Davis, E. P., Sandman, C. A., Sporns, O., O'Donnell, B. F., Buss, C., et al. (2016). Children's intellectual ability is associated with structural network integrity. *NeuroImage, 124*, 550–556.

Lent, R. W., Brown, S. D., & Hackett, G. (1994). Toward a unifying social cognitive theory of career and academic interest, choice, and performance. *Journal of Vocational Behavior, 45*, 79–122.

McCrae, R. R., & Sutin, A. R. (2009). Openness to experience. In M. R. Leary & R. H. Hoyle (Eds.), *Handbook of individual differences in social behavior* (pp. 257–273). New York: Guilford.

Messick, S. (1995). Validity of psychological assessment: Validation of inferences from persons' responses and performances as scientific inquiry into score meaning. *American Psychologist, 50,* 741–749.

Richards, R. (2007). Everyday creativity: Our hidden potential. In R. Richards (Ed.), *Everyday creativity and new views of human nature: Psychological, social, and spiritual perspectives* (pp. 25–53). Washington, DC: American Psychological Association.

Richards, R. (2010). Everyday creativity: Process and way of life—four key issues. In J. C. Kaufman & R. J. Sternberg (Eds.), *The Cambridge handbook of creativity* (pp. 189–215). New York: Cambridge University Press.

Runco, M. A. (2014). *Creativity* (2nd ed.). London, UK: Academic Press.

Runco, M. A., & Acar, S. (2012). Divergent thinking as an indicator of creative potential. *Creativity Research Journal, 24,* 66–75.

Sawyer, R. K. (2012). *Explaining creativity: The science of human innovation* (2nd ed.). New York: Oxford University Press.

Silvia, P. J. (2015). Intelligence and creativity are pretty similar after all. *Educational Psychology Review, 27,* 599–606.

Silvia, P. J., Beaty, R. E., Nusbaum, E. C., Eddington, K. M., Levin-Aspenson, H., & Kwapil, T. R. (2014). Everyday creativity in daily life: An experience-sampling study of "little c" creativity. *Psychology of Aesthetics, Creativity, and the Arts, 8,* 183–188.

Sternberg, R. J. (2006). The nature of creativity. *Creativity Research Journal, 18,* 87–98.

Wallach, M. A., & Kogan, N. (1965). *Modes of thinking in young children: A study of the creativity–intelligence distinction.* New York: Holt, Rinehart, & Winston.

PAUL J. SILVIA *is an associate professor of psychology at the University of North Carolina at Greensboro. He studies creativity assessment and how executive processes shape creative thought.*

ALEXANDER P. CHRISTENSEN *is a graduate student in the Department of Psychology, University of North Carolina at Greensboro. His research focuses on individual differences in creativity and cognition.*

KATHERINE N. COTTER *is a graduate student in the Department of Psychology, University of North Carolina at Greensboro. Her research interests include musical imagery and the psychology of art and aesthetics.*

INDEX

Ability beliefs, fixed, 88–89
Abraham, A., 66
Acar, S., 26, 99, 103, 112
Adamson, R. E., 64
Adaptive disengagement, 93
Adolescence, 74; creative ideation training in, 79–80; creative thinking in, development of, 74–77; neural processes in, development of, 77–79
Affect in Play Scale (APS), 25, 26; preschool version (APS-P), 25
Affective processes, in creative production, 22. *See also* Pretend play, and creativity
Affect symbol system, 24
Agogué, M., 61, 65, 66, 72
Albert, R. S., 87, 98, 99, 101, 103
Alternate Uses Task (AUT), 75, 77
Alvarez, C., 92, 93
Alvarez, G. A., 16
Amabile's Consensual Assessment Technique, 13
Amabile, T. M., 7, 11, 13, 16, 22, 35, 62, 74, 103, 105, 114
American Psychological Association, 11
Anaki, D., 115
Anastasi, A., 11
Andrews-Hanna, J. R., 115
Angello, G., 64, 69
Antonietti, A., 68
Arden, R., 77
Arenberg, D., 36, 99
Aspirational commitment (AC), 90–91
Assessment of creativity, 11–12

Baas, M., 74–76, 78, 81
Bäckström, P., 38
Baer, J., 7, 9–11, 13, 15, 16, 20, 25, 34
Bahleda, M. D., 77
Ballard, C. G., 16
Bandalos, D., 26, 99
Bandura, A., 86, 88, 90
Barbot, B., 8, 10, 12, 14, 17, 33–35, 37, 38, 40, 43, 45, 48, 58
Barrett, H. C., 64, 65
Bartesaghi, N., 68
Bass, M., 22

Beaty, R. E., 14, 67, 69, 113, 115
Beghetto, R. A., 10, 35, 85–90, 94, 95, 113, 116
Benedek, M., 23, 67, 69, 115
Bentler, P. M., 51
Besançon, M., 10, 12, 14, 17, 33–36, 38–40, 45
Bhavnani, R., 27
Big C creativity, 35, 48, 102
Bijvoet-van den Berg, S., 36
Birney, D. P., 34
Block, J., 99, 105
Block, J. H., 99, 105
Bloom, B. S., 15
Bloom's cognitive skills, 15
Boccia, M., 67
Bohlin, G., 38
Bond, T. G., 51
Borst, G., 61–65, 72
Bott, N. T., 79
Brackfleld, S. C., 62
Branje, S. J. T., 37
Brown, S. D., 116
Bunge, S. A., 79
Burns, A. S., 16
Buss, C., 115
Byrne, B. M., 51

Cacciari, C., 66
Camarda, A., 61, 72
Caramelli, P., 68
Cardenas-Iniguez, C., 16
Carlsson. I., 78
Caroff, X., 42
Carter, C. S., 79
Casey, B. J., 74
Cassotti, M., 61, 66, 72
Cayirdag, N., 38
Celano, M. J., 65
Chaiken, S., 74
Chang, P., 16
Chan, K., 37
Charles, R. E., 35–37, 39, 101, 103
Chavez-Eakle, R., 78
Chavez, R. S., 77
Cheng, S., 37
Cheng, Y., 39, 77

Cheung, P. C., 36, 77
Chown, S. M., 101
Christensen, A. P., 111, 119
Christiano, B., 25–27, 99
Christie, J., 28
Christoff, K., 75–76
Chumakova, M. A., 57
Cianci, A. M., 86
Cicogna, P., 66
Clark, P., 27
Claxton, A. F., 36, 39
Cliatt, M. J. P., 79
CM. See Creative mortification (CM)
"Cognification" of play, 25
Cognitive biases, 63, 65
Cognitive flexibility, 74–75
Cognitive persistence, 75
Cognitive processes, in creative production, 22. See also Pretend play, and creativity
Cognitive skills, 15
Cohen, J., 52
Cohen, J. D., 77
Collier, C., 38
Colombo, B., 68
Common Core, and creative thinking skills, 10, 17
Competence development, 86
Confirmatory factor analysis (CFA), 51, 55
Conner, T. S., 113
Conscientiousness, and creativity, 16
Content specific creativity, 10–17
Content standards movement, 10
Conti, R., 13
Coon, H., 13
Cooperberg, M., 27
Copeland, D., 38
Costa, P. T., 36, 99
Cotter, K. N., 111, 119
Cramond, B., 26, 99
Creative achievement, 34
Creative continuance, 89–90, 92–93
Creative-expertise hypothesis, 37
Creative ideas generation. See also Inhibitory control: fixation effect during, 66; inhibitory control and, 65–68
Creative identity, 86
Creative mortification (CM), 86–87, 89, 92–94, 116; aspirational commitment

and, 90–91; creative continuance and, 89–90, 92–93; feedbacks and, 91; fixed ability beliefs and, 88–89; internal attributions of failure and, 88; negative performance outcomes and, 87–88; process model of, 87; shame and, 89; sociocultural context and, 91
Creative outcomes, 74–75
Creative potential, 35, 98, 101, 112 ; and creative achievement, 35; discontinuity of development of, 35–37; optimal-fit view of, 40–41
Creative production: in adulthood, pretend play and, 22; affective processes in, 22; cognitive processes in, 22; pretend play and (see also Pretend play, and creativity)
Creative-thinking skills, 15–16
Creativity, 10, 74, 112; asynchronicity and development of, 37–38; definition of, 34; development of, 10–17, 112–117; discontinuity in development of, 36–38; environmental influences on development of, 38–39; g-factor view, 34; longitudinal research on, 99–103; methodological limitations and artifacts and, 39–40; nature of, 34–35; optimal-fit view, 35, 40–41
Creativity Ability Test (CAT), 75
Creativity-focused education, absence of, 10–12
Creativity Research Journal, 12
Creativity training, domain specificity/generality in, 14–15
Creativity training programs, 12, 17, 117
Crockenberg, S. B., 11
Crone, E. A., 36, 39, 62, 65, 67, 73, 75, 76, 78–80, 84, 104
Cropley, A. J., 101
Cropley, D. H., 117
Cross-cultural invariance of creativity ratings, study on, 47–49; analytical approach, 51; confirmatory multigroup factor analysis, 53–55; Creative Stories task, 50–51; discussion, 55–58; interrater reliabilities, 50, 52; Many-Facet Rasch modeling, 52–53; participants, 49–50; results, 51–55
Cruz Fuentes, C., 78
Csikszentmihalyi, M., 11, 12, 24, 99

Culture, role of, in creativity, 48, 103, 117. *See also* Cross-cultural invariance of creativity ratings, study on

Dahlman, S., 38
Dahl, R. E., 62, 79, 80
Dai, D. Y., 38
Dajani, S., 16
Dalmasso, C., 66
Damian, R. I., 38
Dansky, J., 24, 26, 28
Darbellay, F., 98
Daubman, K., 22, 24
Davies, D., 38
Davis, E. P., 115
Davranche, K., 68, 69
Deary, I. J., 113
De Dreu, C. K., 36, 39, 78
De Dreu, C. K. W., 22, 62, 65, 67, 73–76, 78–81, 84, 104
Deegan, M. P., 93
Defeyter, M. A., 65
DeHaan, R. J., 65
Deliberate-analytic system, 63
DeMunn, N. W., 92
De Neys, W., 63, 64
Dermen, D., 76
de Souza, L. C., 68
Diamond, A., 62, 69
Dietrich, A., 62, 64, 67, 68, 69, 75, 77, 99
Differential facet analysis (DFF), 51
Digby, R., 38
Dilalla, L., 27
Dilley, A. E., 85, 95
Divergent thinking (DT), 35–36, 75, 101; and creativity, 25–28; individual differences in, 36; slumps and peak, 36; systematic maturational declines, 36
Divergent thinking tests, 25–26, 100, 105
Dolan, C. V., 76
Domain-based skills and knowledge, for creativity, 10, 37
Domain specificity of creativity, 12–17
Donohue, S., 79
Dore, R., 25, 26, 28
Dow, G., 101
Dow, G. T., 14, 15

Driagina, V., 56
DT. *See* Divergent thinking (DT)
Dual Pathway to Creativity Model, 74–75
Dual process model of creativity, 62–64
Dubois, B., 68
Dumas, D., 40
Dunbar, K. N., 40
Duncker, K., 64
Dunning, D., 90
Dweck, C. S., 88, 91

Ebner, F., 67, 69
Eckstrand, K., 74
Eckstrom, R. B., 76
Eddington, K. M., 113
Edl, S., 67
Edwards, D., 56
Einert, M., 79
Eisenman, R., 105
Engelhart, M. D., 15
Engle, R. W., 16
Erez, M., 48
Ericsson, K. A., 86
Executive functioning tests, 113
External-other attributions, 88

Family environment, and creative potential development, 38, 103
Faust, M., 115
Fearon, D. D., 38
Fehr, K., 25
Fein, G., 22, 24, 25
Feist, G. J., 16
Fink, A., 67, 69, 115
Finkelstein, S. R., 90
Finke, R. A., 65, 74
Fishbach, A., 90
Fissell, K., 79
Flow experience, in creative production, 24
Folley, B. S., 78
Förster, J., 75, 76
Fournier, M., 68, 69
Fox, C. M., 51
Frans, Ö, 38
Franz, F., 67, 69
Frederick, S., 62
Freeman, S., 28
French, J. W., 76

Freud, S., 24
Fried, D. E., 16
Friedman, R. S., 75, 76
Functional fixedness, 64. *See also* Inhibitory control; developmental studies of, 65; overcoming of, in older children and adults, 65
Functional magnetic resonance imaging (fMRI), 77, 104
Furst, F. J., 15

Gabrieli, J. D. E., 16
Garcia-Reyna, J., 78
Gardner, H., 12, 98
Garel, K. L. A., 16
Gaynor J. L. R., 103
Gentile, C. A., 11
German, T. P., 64, 65
Gerris, J. R. M., 37
Gestalt Completion Task (GCT), 76, 77
Getzels, J.W., 114
Gibson, C., 78
Giedd, J. N., 65
Gitlin-Weiner, K., 25
Global-self attributions, 88
Goddard, C., 56
Goel, V., 79
Gogtay, N., 74
Goldfarb, P., 62
Goode, A., 79
Gordon, A., 75–76
Graf-Guerrero, A., 78
Grahn, J. A., 16
Grazioplene, R., 77
Griffing, P., 27
Griffith, D. A., 48
Grigorenko, E. L., 37, 38, 43, 47–50, 58, 59
Grossman-McKee, A., 22, 25, 26
Gryskiewicz, N. D., 103, 105
Guignard, J., 38
Guilford, J. P., 22, 26, 75, 78–79, 101, 104
Guimarães, H. C., 68

Hackett, G., 116
Haenschel, C., 77
Hambrick, D. Z., 16
Hampshire, A., 16
Hare, T. A., 74
Harman, M. H., 76

Harrington, D. M., 99, 105
Harrison, T. L., 16
Hart, L., 49, 50
Hatchuel, A., 65
Hay, P., 38
Heene, M., 67, 69
Hehman, E., 93
Helson, R., 98, 99
Hennessey, B. A., 16
Hicks, K. L., 16
Hidi, S., 90
Hill, W. H., 15
Hirshorn, E. A., 79
Hocevar, D., 104
Hoffmann, J., 25–28
Hoicka, E., 36
Hong, D. W-C., 79
Hong, E., 37, 86, 99
Hopkins, E., 25, 26, 28
Hoppe, K. D., 101
Houdé, O., 61–67, 72
Howard, A., 92, 93
Howard, R. G., 16
Howe, A., 38
Hui, A. N., 37
Hui, D. C., 37
Huizinga, M., 76
Hunter, S. R., 38
Hunt, J. McV., 101
Hutt, C., 27
Hu, W., 36, 38

Illies, J. J., 105
Inhibitory control, 62, 68–69; and creative ideas generation, 65–68; and creative problem solving, 64–65; dual process theory and, 62–64; role in reasoning and decision making, 62
Insight problem solving, 14–15
Insight solutions, and noninsight solutions, 76
Insight tasks, 76
Interdisciplinary thinking, 16
Intrinsic motivation, creativity and, 16
Intuitive-heuristic system, 63
Ip, H. M., 39, 77
Isen, A., 22, 24
Ivcevic, Z., 13

Jackson, P. W., 114
Jaeger, G., 99

Jaeger, G. J., 48
Jarvin, L., 49, 50
Jauk, E., 23, 67, 69, 115
Jindal-Snape, D., 38
Johnson, C., 76, 80
Johnson, L., 27
Joliot, M., 67
Jolles, D. D., 62, 65, 67, 78–80, 104
Jones, J. M., 93
Jones, R. M., 74
Jung, R. E., 77, 115

Kabani, N. J., 74
Kahneman, D., 63
Kane, M. J., 16
Kanso, R., 62, 64, 67, 69, 75, 77
Karbach, J., 79
Kasari, C., 28
Kaufman, J., 10, 25
Kaufman, J. C., 10, 11, 16, 22, 35, 90, 94, 113
Kaufman, S. B., 115, 116
Kaugars, A., 25
Kaugars, A. S., 25, 26
Kazakçi, A., 65
Keating, D. P., 80
Kenett, Y. N., 115
Kharkhurin, A. V., 103
Kienitz, E., 79
Kim, D. J., 115
Kim, K. H., 11, 26, 75, 81
Kleibeuker, S. W., 36, 39, 62, 65, 67, 73, 75, 76, 78–80, 84, 104
Klein, H. J., 86
Kliegel, M., 79
Klingberg, T., 79
Kluckhon, C., 48
Koch, G. G., 52
Kogan, N., 24, 104, 114
Kohn, N. W., 62
Koolschijn, P. C. M. P., 62, 65, 67, 78–80, 104
Kornilova, T. V., 47, 57, 59
Kornilov, S. A., 47, 50, 57, 59
Koschutnig, K., 67, 69
Kovecses, Z., 56
Krapp, A., 90
Krasnor, I., 22
Krathwohl, D. R., 15
Kray, J., 79
Kris, E., 24

Kroeber, A. L., 48
Kruger, J., 90
Kwapil, T. R., 113
Kwiatkowski, J., 49, 50
Kyle, N. L., 101

Lala, N., 16
Lalonde, F. M., 65
Landis, J. R., 52
Lau, S., 36, 77
Lautrey, J., 38, 101
Lee, K., 62, 69
Lee, N. R., 65
Leitner, J. B., 93
Le Masson, P., 66
Lenroot, R., 74
Lent, R. W., 116
Lerch, J. P., 74
Leritz, L. E., 12
Lerner, M., 25, 26, 28
Levin-Aspenson, H., 113
Levorato. M. C., 66
Levy, R., 68
Lewis, M., 88, 89, 91, 92
Liberman, N., 75, 76
Lieberman, J. N., 26
Lillard, A., 25, 26, 28
Lim,W., 28
Linacre, J. M., 51, 52
Lindauer, M. S., 98
Lubart, T., 10, 34, 35, 38, 40, 48, 74, 101
Lubart, T. I., 7, 12, 14, 17, 33–36, 38, 39, 42, 43, 45, 62, 86
Lubin, A., 67
Luna, B., 74

MacKinnon, D., 98, 105
Many-Facet   Rasch   Measurement (MFRM) model, 51, 52–53, 55
Marathe, D., 38
March, J. G., 100
Masson, P., 65
Masters, G. N., 52
Matchstick   Problem   Tasks   (MPT), 78–79
Mathews-Morgan, J., 26, 99
Mayer, R. E., 14, 15
Mayseless, N., 68
McBride-Chang, C., 39, 77
McCarthy, K. A., 104
McCollum, V. A., 12, 14

McCormick, M. J., 63, 65
McCrae, R. R., 36, 99, 115
McWilliams, J., 36, 38
Mednick, S., 104
Mednick, S. A., 77
Merrotsy, P., 102
Messick, S., 113
Milgram, R. M., 86, 99, 105
Millar, G., 26, 99
Miller, E. K., 77
Mills, K. L., 77
Moody, Z., 98
Moore, M., 28, 99
Mourgues, C., 38, 48, 58
Mullineaux, P., 27
Mumford,M. D., 12
Murphy, M., 103

Negative affect, in pretend play, 24
Neubauer, A., 23
Neubauer, A. C., 67, 69
Neuroimaging, 77
Newman, T., 49, 50
Nijstad, B. A., 22, 74–76, 78, 81
Niu, W., 39
Nori, R., 67
Nouri, R., 48
Nowicki, G., 22, 24
Nusbaum, E. C., 14, 67, 69, 113

O'Donnell, B. F., 115
O'Hearn, K., 74
Okuda, S. M., 104
O'Neil H. F. Jr., 37
Ordanini, A., 48
Overgaauw, S., 80
Owen, A. M., 16

Padmanabhan, A., 74
Palermo, L., 67
Palmiero, M., 67
Palmquist, C., 25, 26, 28
Pannells, T. C., 36, 39
Paparella, T., 28
Papousek, I., 67
Paraskevopoulos, J., 101
Park, S., 78
Patel, T. N., 64
"The path of least resistance" model, 65, 66
Patterson, M. J., 65, 66

Pavlenko, A., 56
Peng, Y., 37
Pepler, D., 22
Performance assessments, domain generality in, 13
Pfennig, L., 79
Piaget, J., 99
Piccardi, L., 67
Pineau, A., 66
Play facilitation sessions, 28
Plucker, J., 25, 28
Plucker, J. A., 10, 13, 35, 36, 38
Poirel, N., 65, 66
Pollard, K., 16
Positive affect, in pretend play, 24
Prefrontal cortex (PFC), 76–80
Pretend play, and creativity, 22, 99; affective processes in, 23; cognitive processes in, 23; correlational studies, 26; divergent thinking and, 25–26; empirical evidence, 25–26; experimental studies, 28–29; future directions, 29; longitudinal studies, 26–28; relationship between, 23, 24
Pretend play measures, 25
Pretz, J. E., 12, 14, 22
Pruzek, R. M., 38
Psychology of Aesthetics, Creativity, and the Arts, 10

Qin, Y., 79
Quintin, E.-M., 79

Rabkin, L., 105
Radel, R., 68, 69
Randi, J., 43
Redick, T. S., 16
Reflective abstraction, 99
Reishofer, G., 67, 69
Reiter-Palmon, R., 103, 105
Remote Associates Task (RAT), 76–77
Renninger, K. A., 90
Reyna, V. F., 63, 65
Reynolds, G. O., 16
Rhoads, P. A., 36, 39
Richards, R., 113
Rietzschel, E. F., 74–76, 81
Risberg, J., 78
Robins, A., 25–27, 99
Robinson, M. D., 67
Robins, R. W., 88, 89, 91, 94

Rodriguez, E., 77
Root-Bernstein, M., 24
Root-Bernstein, R., 24
Roskes, M., 78
Rossi, S., 63, 67
Roux, F., 77
Royalty, A., 79
Rubera, G., 48
Rubin, K., 25
Rudowicz, E., 103
Rummo, J., 26
Runco, M., 22, 26, 27, 28
Runco, M. A., 12, 35, 36, 37, 38, 39, 48,
    77, 97–105, 109, 112
Russell, J. A., 56
Russ, S., 22, 23, 24–26, 25, 26, 27, 28, 99
Russ, S. W., 21, 22, 25–27, 26, 28, 32, 99

Saggar, M., 79
Sakamoto, S. O., 101
Salzberger, T., 55
Sandgrund, A., 25
Sandman, C. A., 115
Santa-Donato, G., 43
Sawyer, K., 11, 22
Sawyer, R. K., 114
Saxon, T. F., 38
Schacter, D. L., 115
Schaefer, C., 25
Schafer, E., 25, 28, 99
Scheff, T. J., 89
Schel, M. A., 65, 78, 80
Scott, G., 12
Seah, Y. Z., 34
Sedooka, A., 98
Seijts, G. H., 86
Self-generated thought, 23, 99
Shamay-Tsoory, S. G., 68
Shame, 89
Shaw, J. M., 79
Shaw, P., 74
Shen, J., 38
Sherwood, J. M., 79
Shipstead, Z., 16
Shmukler, D., 27
Sifonis, C. M., 65, 66
Silk, E. M., 79
Silvia, P. J., 14, 67, 69, 111, 113–115, 119
Simonelli, L., 68
Simonton, D. K., 34, 37, 38, 40
Singer, D. G., 23, 24

Singer, D. L., 26
Singer, J. L., 23, 24
Singer, W., 77
Sinkovics, R. R., 55
Sireteanu, R., 77
Smith, E., 25, 26, 28
Smith, R., 75–76
Smith, S. M., 62, 65, 74
Smith, W. R., 101
Snow, F. B., 92
Snowy Picture Task (SPT), 76, 77
Sporns, O., 115
Steffen, G., 98
Steinberg, L., 74, 80
Stenger, V. A., 79
Stenton, R., 16
Sternberg, R. J., 7, 11, 12, 22, 34, 48–50,
    62, 74, 86, 114
Stevenson, C. E., 80
Storm, B. C., 64, 69
Stroop interference effect, 67
Sue-Chan, C., 37
Suler, J., 22
Sullivan, M. W., 88, 89, 91, 92
Sutin, A. R., 115
Svensen, E., 104
Symbolic play, 28

Talent loss, 86
Tamnes, C. K., 77
Tan, C., 103
Tan, M., 37, 38, 43, 48, 58
Tan, X., 38
Teixeira, A. L., 68
Thompson-Schill, S. H., 79
Thompson, T. W., 16
Thurston, B. J., 104
Tinio, P. P. L., 34, 35
Torrance, E. P., 7, 11, 36, 38, 39, 75, 100,
    104
Torrance Tests, 11, 66
Tracy, J. L., 88, 89, 91, 94
Trope, Y., 74

Uhlhaas, P. J., 77

Valtcheva, A., 38
Vandenberg, B., 25
Van der Aar, L., 80
van der Molen, M.W., 76
Vanderputte, K., 63

Van Duijvenvoorde, A. C., 80
Van Gelder, E., 64
van Leijenhorst, L., 79
van Lieshout, C. F. M., 37
Vartanian, O., 67, 79
Vaugier, V., 78
Verbal creative idea generation, neurode-
   velopmental changes of, 78
Vygotsky, L. S., 24

Wallace, C., 24–27
Wallace, G. L., 65
Wallach, M. A., 34, 104, 114
Ward, T. B., 65, 66, 74
Waskom, M. L., 16
Weil, B., 65
Weiner, B., 88
Weiss, E. M., 67
Weldon, R. B., 63, 65
Wendelken, C., 79
Wendt, P. E., 78
White, S. L., 65

Wierzbicka, A., 56
Wilbrecht, L., 76, 80
Wilce, J. M., 56
Wilhelms, E. A., 63, 65
Wilkins, R. W., 115
Willingham, D., 16
Windmann, S., 66
Winter, R., 16
Wolsink, I., 78
Wright, B. D., 52
Wu, C. H., 39, 77

Yeung, D. Y., 37
Yi, X., 36, 38
Yue, X. D., 103

Zabelina, D. L., 67
Zbikowski, S. M., 16
Zenasni, F., 35, 43
Zhengdao, Y., 56
Zinke, K., 79
Zuo, L., 26, 99